# GAUGUIN

## *His Life and Complete Works*

JOAN MINGUET

LONGMEADOW
P  R  E  S  S

© 1995 Creación y Edición
Multimedia, S.A. Barcelona

For this present English
language edition:
Todtri Productions Limited,
New York

ISBN: 0-681-10477-5

Printed in Spain by
Fournier Artes Gráficas, S.A.

**Editor:**

Clotilde de Bellegarde

**Designer:**

Luis F. Balaguer

**Editorial Assistants:**

José Antonio Vázquez

Patricia Núñez Millieri

Rosa Vallribera i Fius

Albert Pujol Gámiz

**English Translation:**

Adrian Harris / Discobole

**Design Assistants:**

Manuel Domingo Pérez

Miguel Ortíz Català

**Publishing Assistant:**

Monserrat Juan Peña

Paul Gauguin was born in Paris, in Rue Notre-Dame-de-Lorette, on 7 June 1848, under the sign of Gemini. The previous year, the painter's mother, Aline Marie Chazal, had had a daughter, Marie. Mysteriously, Gauguin conceals this sister in all his memoirs and in his artistic work. On 8 August 1849, when Gauguin was just fourteen months old, his family took ship for Peru, since the painter's father Clovis Gauguin, who was a journalist on the *National*, intended to found a newspaper in Lima. In those days, the voyage to Peru was extremely difficult and Clovis Gauguin, who already suffered from heart disease, could not stand up to it. In the Straits of Magellan, off Chile, he died "as a result of a ruptured aneurysm," in Gauguin's own words.

On arrival in Peru, the Gauguin family went to live in Lima, in the house of Pío de Tristán de Moscoso, the painter's great uncle. Thus, the future artist's early childhood was spent in an exotic landscape. Mid-nineteenth-century Lima was a rapidly-expanding town, but it far from resembled a modern European city, and it must still have had many evident features of the primitive indigenous world of South America. Gauguin must have felt influenced by those early years spent in Peru. In one of his autobiographical writings he said of this period, "I remember that time very well, I remember our house and many things that happened... I can still see the little negro girl, whose duty it was to carry to church the little carpet on which we used to kneel to pray. I can also see our Chinese servant, who was so good at ironing the clothes. It was he who found me in the grocery store where I was sitting sucking sugar cane between two barrels of molasses, while my mother was desperately sending everyone looking for me everywhere."

In the autumn of 1854 the Gauguin family returned to France and made their home in Orléans. This move was prompted by Paul and Marie's paternal grandfather's offer to advance a part of their inheritance. Guillaume Gauguin, the grandfather, died shortly afterwards, on 9 April 1855, and the family decided to nominate Isidore Gauguin, the painter's paternal uncle, as the children's guardian. Between 1854 and 1861 then, Gauguin lived in an atmosphere that was radically different from that of his early childhood, in the riverside city of Orléans, with an enormous European cultural tradition that was a far cry from the primitivism and exoticism of mid-nineteenth-century Peru. We know

*Eugène Henri Paul Gauguin, the son of Pierre Guillaume Clovis Gauguin and Aline Marie Chazal, was born on 7 June 1848 in this house in the Rue Notre-Dame-de-Lorette in Paris. He lived there just fourteen months, before his family moved to Peru.*

*In 1862, Gauguin began his preparatory studies to enter naval school. Having failed to do so, he joined the navy in December 1865 and boarded the* Luzitano *in Le Havre bound for Rio de Janeiro.*

that at least from 1859 he went to school at the junior seminary in La Chapelle-Saint-Mesmin, near Orléans.

In 1861, Aline Gauguin set up in Paris as a dressmaker and commenced a relationship with the Arosa family. Paul Gauguin rejoined his mother in 1862, as he was to attend the Loriol Institute in Paris, for preliminary studies for entry into the naval college. In 1864 he spent his last academic year in Orléans.

On failure to obtain a place in the naval college, in December 1865, he joined the merchant navy as an officer cadet on the *Luzitano*, a three-master on which he made three voyages to Rio de Janeiro, each lasting four months. In October 1866 he set sail again, this time on board the *Chili*, on a voyage that lasted three and a half months and which was to take him back to Pacific waters and to the Chilean and Peruvian cities that must have reminded him of his early years in these lands. While ashore during this voyage, Gauguin learned of the death of his mother on 7 July 1867. When Paul Gauguin returned to Paris, his mother had been dead for a little over five months. Paul and his sister Marie had been made the only heirs and their new guardian was Gustave Arosa, a photographer and collector of modern painting. In January 1868 Gauguin was finally able to join the navy and served on board the corvette *Jérôme-Napoléon*, in which he voyaged round the Mediterranean and to the Scandinavian countries until 1871. In 1872, having given up his sea-faring life, he was recommended by Gustave Arosa and began to work successfully as a stockbroker in Paul Bertin's business. It seemed that Gauguin's life, after a period of considerable excitement, roving the world on voyages to exotic lands, was beginning to take a more conventional course.

In 1873 he married Mette Gad, a Dane whom he had met through Gustave Arosa, who was a witness at the wedding along with Paul Bertin and Oscar Fahle, secretary of the Danish consulate. He had five children by Mette Gad: Emil, Aline, Clovis, Jean-René and Paul. This life, so peaceful in comparison with the rambunctiousness of the foregoing years, nonetheless began to be marked by a new factor that was to have enormous consequences: his growing interest in painting. It seems that already in 1874, the year his first son was born, he had done a few drawings. What is certain is that in 1876 he made his public debut as a painter: in the Paris Salon of that year he exhibited a work entitled *Thicket in Viroflay (Seine-et-Oise).* Although painting still did not have the dominating position it was later to have in his life, it was entering slowly but decisively into Gauguin's calculations.

In the following years he had several other jobs in banking and two more children were born, who were named after their paternal grandparents: Aline in 1877, and Clovis two years later. However, Gauguin's artistic vocation was becoming ever more marked. In 1877 he went to live in Vaugirard, where the sculptor Bouillot taught him the principles of his art. His solid financial situation enabled him to form a good collection of modern art. What is more, in 1879 at the invitation of Pissarro and Degas, he took part unofficially in the fourth Impressionist exhibition. From the letters that have been preserved between Gauguin and Pissarro we know that in this period Paul Gauguin was in fact in contact with several Impressionist painters: Degas, Renoir, and Manet, as well as Pissarro himself.

This contact with the Impressionists was to become more intense, first as a collector of the group's paintings, and later as a painter. The summer of 1879 was spent for the first time in Pontoise with his friend Pissarro, from whom he learnt landscape technique. With his easel on his back, Gauguin painted landscapes that captured the outdoors, meticulously representational using small brushstrokes.

Under the influence of another of the masters of the time, Degas, who was a friend for a long time and for whom he always felt admiration,

*On 22 November 1873, Paul Gauguin married Mette Gad at the Town Hall of the Ninth District of Paris. The religious ceremony was held at the Lutheran Evangelist Church of the Redemption.*

he also painted interiors. Good examples of these are two canvases with female figures: *Mette Sewing*, in which Gauguin expresses to us through his wife the peacefulness of his daily life, and *Suzanne Sewing* or *Nude Study*, a female nude that was highly regarded by the writer Joris-Karl Huysmans. The author of *À Rebours* went so far as to say of this painting, "I venture to state that, of all the contemporary painters who work with the nude, nobody has so far struck a note of such vehement reality."

Gauguin was pleased at the promising beginnings of his artistic career. He took part in the fifth, sixth, and seventh Impressionist exhibitions, between 1880 and 1882. Shortly before this last exhibition, in January 1882, there was a crash on the stock exchange and Gauguin found himself without a job. In spite of the dramatic situation, Gauguin felt that this was a chance to devote himself entirely to painting. In the face of this crisis the Gauguin family left Paris and moved to Rouen in early 1884, in the hope of being able to live more cheaply. In the meantime, the two last children had been born: Jean-René in 1881, and Paul in 1883. A revealing fact: on the birth certificate of this last child Gauguin is not described as a stock-exchange agent, but as a painter. However, although Gauguin's letters show that he was confident of success as an artist, realities had to be faced and his financial situation became more and more precarious. Finally, in November 1884 Paul Gauguin moved to Denmark, his wife's native country, where she and the children had gone a few weeks earlier. Here he became a sailcloth agent for Scandinavia. But things did not improve and in 1885 Gauguin decided to return to Paris, accompanied by his son Clovis. Mette Gauguin remained in Copenhagen with the other children and

*Beyond doubt, Pissarro and Degas are the painters who had the greatest influence on Gauguin. In this double portrait of Gauguin and Pissarro (Louvre Museum, Paris), the master did a more incisive sketch of the pupil, whose lines are not so clear. From 1879, Gauguin painted regularly at Pissarro's side and enjoyed the benefit of his advice.*

tried to make a living by giving French classes. Between June 1885 and mid-1886, Gauguin accepted any job that would enable him to survive, such as posting advertising bills for five francs a day; but he went on painting, as well as reestablishing some contacts. He even took part in the eighth and final Impressionist exhibition, opened in 1886. His great blossoming as a painter, however, was not to take place until July 1886, when having left his son Clovis in a boarding school, he decided to leave for Brittany.

## GAUGUIN IN PONT-AVEN

Having arrived in Pont-Aven, a small town in Finisterre, Gauguin wrote to his wife, "I have finally found the money for my journey to Brittany and I am living here on credit. Hardly anyone here is French; they are all foreigners: three Danes, Hagborg's brother, and many Americans. My painting is provoking a lot of discussion and I must say that the Americans quite approve of it. There is a hope for the 'future'. I am doing lots of sketches, and you would hardly recognize my painting. I hope to be able to get on this season." The enthusiasm that underlies these words was natural. After those periods of depression between Paris and Rouen, Rouen and Copenhagen, between Copenhagen and Paris again, Paul Gauguin was for the first time able to express himself as a painter in the full sense of the word. Little by little, during the three short months of his stay in the Gloanec inn in Pont-Aven, his output extended from the landscapes that were still Impressionist in tone, such as in *Washerwomen in Pont-Aven*, to works containing the first signs of what was to become his distinctive style.

*Gauguin, the second on the right sitting on the ground, in front of the Pension Gloanec. He wrote to Mette about it in a letter from Pont-Aven in June 1886: "It is a pity we did not come to Britanny before; in the hotel we are paying 65 francs a month for full board."*

*In this pencil sketch, Gauguin drew himself in a cap and Charles Laval in a hat. When painting the Breton women with their white wimples and clogs, Gauguin concentrated on suggesting an environment.*

When painting the Breton women with their distinctive white wimples, Paul Gauguin concentrated on evoking, on suggesting, a moment or a situation, rather than describing, recording reality, as a true Impressionist would have done, or as he would have done himself a few years previously.

In Pont-Aven, before his return to Paris, several things happened that were to produce developments in the coming months. He met the painter Émile Bernard, a remarkable character with whom he was to work closely, albeit not without moments of tension, during his second stay in Brittany. He also met Charles Laval, another painter with whom, a few months later, he was to undertake an exotic voyage to Martinique. And in essence, he laid down the vital and artistic foundations for his subsequent development as a painter, among which should be mentioned his rapid introduction to the language of ceramics, which he owed to Ernest Chaplet. In ceramics he found a possibility for immediacy, tangibility, and tactility in the development of forms that, according to Françoise Cachin, for him meant a return to the origins of art and to his childhood in Peru where his mother had assembled a good collection of ceramics.

Gauguin's life in Paris was not a quiet one. At the same time as a reconciliation with Degas after a brief period of enmity, he broke resoundingly in an incident in the Café de la Nouvelle-Athènes with Paul Signac and his old friend Camille Pissarro. As if he had foreseen that his painting was soon to distance itself from Impressionist precepts, Gauguin broke off relations with some of the most orthodox representatives of the current artistic tendency, but he remained in contact with Parisian cultural life and through *Le Figaro littéraire*, he followed Jean Moréas' Symbolist Manifesto.

In April 1887 Mette came to Paris to collect her son Clovis and to take back with her some of Gauguin's paintings with the intention of selling them to make ends meet. The same month, Gauguin set sail with the painter Charles Laval for Panama. In a letter to Mette, Gauguin revealed his most intimate desires for the journey, "What I want to do above all is to get away from Paris, which is a desert for a poor man. My reputation as an artist is growing by the day, but in the meantime I sometimes go three days without eating; which not only damages my health, but also my 'energy'. I want to recover this energy, and I am going to Panama to live 'wild'." Gauguin was fleeing for the first time, although it seems it was not purely a creative flight, but rather the fruit of the need to escape his personal situation in Paris. However, the journey to Panama was beset by difficulties, illness, and penury, and Gauguin was obliged to work for a time on the construction of the Panama Canal. In early June he sailed from Panama for Martinique, in the Caribbean, still accompanied by Laval.

There, undoubtedly, he found landscapes and a way of life that took him back to his childhood in Peru and to the lands he travelled in his seafaring youth. His stay in Martinique was a brief one, since in July he became seriously ill with dysentery and malaria, forcing him to return to France in haste in October 1887. Nonetheless, in those few short weeks, Gauguin took a giant step towards the creation of his own painting style. He found there an environment that was replete with creative suggestions. In a letter to his wife, dated June 1887, Gauguin vividly expressed his enthusiasm, "We have now moved into a negro cabin, in a paradise near the isthmus. Below us, the sea, fringed with coconut palms; above us, all manner of fruit trees, twenty-five minutes from the town. Negro men and women are going by all day, talking incessantly and singing creole songs. Don't imagine this becomes monotonous; on the contrary, it's very varied. I cannot tell you the enthusiasm I feel for life in the French colonies, and I am sure you would feel the same. The great richness of nature and the climate, which is warm, but with cool spells from time to time."

*The primitivism, ingenuity, and simplification of forms in the sculpture of the Breton wayside crucifixes is a summary of Gauguin's artistic aspirations. He drew inspiration from one to paint* The Green Christ.

On arrival in Paris, Gauguin went to stay in the home of his old friend and associate Émile Schuffenecker. There he met Daniel de Monfreid, who was to play an important role in his future stays in Polynesia, as well as the Van Gogh brothers. He had already met Vincent Van Gogh in Paris in 1886, and now they gave each other one of their paintings and began a close friendship. He established commercial relations with the merchant Theo Van Gogh which brought him a substantial sum of money, since Theo bought from him a number of ceramic items and several paintings, including one painted in Martinique, *Under the Mangos*, for which he paid four hundred francs. After the penury he had been going through, these sales were a great relief to Gauguin and enabled him to return to Brittany, a return that was to represent a decisive step towards the formation of his new artistic conception. In fact, early in 1888 Gauguin went back to the Gloanec inn in Pont-Aven. "I love Brittany, and the wildness, the primitiveness I find there. When I hear my clogs clacking on the granite, I hear the sound, dull and blunt, but powerful, that I am looking for in my painting," he wrote to Schuffenecker. In Pont-Aven, Gauguin once again met some of the painters he had known during his previous stay in Brittany. But this time the meeting was to have great cultural significance, because in Pont-Aven a new pictorial conception was born, known as Synthetism or the Pont-Aven school, led by Paul Gauguin and Émile Bernard and involving, to a

greater or lesser extent, Émile Schuffenecker, Charles Laval, Louis Anquetin, Cuno Amiet, Henri Moret, and Paul Sérusier, among others. This new conception is hinted at in the canvas *Breton Women in a Meadow* which Émile Bernard painted during the summer of 1888 and was taken to its ultimate consequences by Gauguin in his subsequent work. Synthetism sought to simplify forms, wanted the painting to capture the idea – the synthesis of the creative process rather than a description of the exterior reality. To this end it used thick lines, dark strokes that limited shapes and created a compartmentalized structure (for this reason the school is also known as Cloisonnism). These compartments, or *cloisons*, are filled with large areas of flat color, without gradations and without shadows. In Synthetist painting, traditional perspective ceases to be fundamental to the representation. The aim of the painting is not now limited to the reproduction of objects, but consists of the expression of ideas by way of a special language. Gauguin, it seems, quickly entered into this conception, so far removed from his Impressionist origins. "Do not copy nature too much," he advised his friend Émile Schuffenecker, and went on, "art is an abstraction; draw it out of nature, dreaming of it, and think more about the creative process than the result."

Gauguin did not leave Pont-Aven until October 1888. By then, he had fallen in love with Madeleine Bernard, his friend Émile's sister, but

Vincent Painting Sunflowers. *Gauguin, November 1888 (Van Gogh Museum, Amsterdam). In his memoirs, Gauguin says of Vincent: "He seemed to have a presentiment of everything that was inside him, hence all that series of suns on suns in full sunlight."*

she did not return his affections, since she was attracted to Charles Laval. Gauguin meanwhile subsisted from the sales Theo Van Gogh managed to make of his ceramics and paintings. Relations with the Van Gogh brothers became closer and closer, and finally Gauguin agreed to move to Arles where Vincent Van Gogh was working. Theo, no doubt motivated by the wish for his brother to have company and to be able to work intensely alongside another painter, suggested to Gauguin that he buy all his output in return for his staying in Arles. Paul accepted the proposal, and thus began one of the most legendary encounters between two of the most conspicuous representatives of the history of modern painting.

## FROM ARLES TO TAHITI

It should be stressed that while the friendship between Gauguin and Van Gogh was exhausting in its intensity, it was also a very rich one. There seemed to be a strong creative attraction between them. And at the same time, no less of a rejection. Again, as in his first residence in Pont-Aven and his fleeting visit to Martinique, Gauguin's stay in Arles was a brief one, lasting a little over two months, from 23 October to 26 December 1888. In spite of its brevity, Gauguin's period in Provence gave his painting a new impetus. The relations between the two artists must have been tense. Gauguin admitted this tension in a letter to Émile Bernard, then a friend of both painters, "Here in Arles I feel completely bewildered, everything seems so small, so petty, the surroundings and the people. Vincent and I can hardly agree about anything, least of all about painting. He admires Daumier, Daubigny, Ziem, and the great Theodore Rousseau, who mean nothing to me. On the other hand, he loathes Ingres, Rafael, Degas, and everyone that I admire... He likes my paintings very much, but while I am doing them, he always finds fault about something or other." Gauguin defined himself as a Primitive and Van Gogh, in a tone not free from scorn, as a Romantic. It seems that the temptation to leave Arles was an ever-present one and only the pressure, one might almost say blackmail, of Theo Van Gogh prevented him from doing so. On 23 December 1888 the relation between the two painters became traumatic. Gauguin told his version of the events in his book of memoirs *Avant et après*: "In the last part of my stay, Vincent became excessively brusque and noisy, then silent. Some nights I surprised Vincent, awake, approaching my bed." What is clear is that that night just before Christmas, after dinner, Van Gogh tried to attack Gauguin with an open razor in the streets of Arles. Gauguin fended off the attack, moved into a hotel, and decided to move away. The following morning, however, he found a clamorous crowd of gendarmes and others around the house where the two painters had lived together. Van Gogh had cut off one of his ears at the base. "It must have taken him a long time to stop the bleeding," wrote Gauguin, "because the next day there were many wet towels on the floor in the two ground-floor rooms. There were bloodstains in both rooms and on the staircase that led up to our bedroom." That very morning he sent a telegram to Theo asking him to come and look after his brother, and with Vincent in hospital, they both returned to Paris two days later.

In spite of the legendary, mythical nature of Vincent Van Gogh's self-mutilation, and in spite of the obscure part Gauguin might have played in these horrifying events, the fact is that for him the time he spent with the "madman with the red hair" must have magnetized to a certain extent, his aesthetic aspirations. Gauguin, not without irony, affirmed that the problems he had suffered in his family and artistic life were not comparable with the mental anguish his colleague suffered, and assessed his encounter with Van Gogh as follows: "When I arrived in Arles, Vincent was in search of himself, while I, much older than he, was a mature man. I owe something to Vincent; that is, apart from the awareness of having been useful to him, the consolidation of my previous artistic ideas, along with the fact that I am able to remind myself, at difficult moments, that there is always someone worse off than yourself."

In 1889 Gauguin lived between Paris and Pont-Aven, but tired of the tiny village, he moved a few kilometers away to Le Pouldu, a fishing village where he was better able to concentrate on the evocation of Breton landscape and culture. Various artists with Synthetist ideas had gathered there: Émile Bernard, who was soon to accuse the painter of appropriating his artistic poetry; Meyer de Haan, with whom Gauguin decorated the dining room of the Hôtel Marie Henry in Le Pouldu, where they usually ate and slept; Paul Sérusier, with whom he also shared the pension from the end of June; and Armand Seguin among others.

Meanwhile, he exhibited several works in two important exhibitions: in February in the Salon des XX in Brussels, and in the exhibition of paintings by the Groupe Impressionniste et Synthétiste, held between June and October in the Café des Arts in the 1889 Universal Exposition in the Champ-de-Mars. This exhibition led to Gauguin's being discovered, in a sense, by some French intellectuals and painters. This was before Gauguin had revealed any of the works he had in mind at that time during his latest stay in Brittany. In fact, in those months Gauguin was painting works of exceptional calibre, prototypes of the revolution that was to take place in his work in the tropics. *The Yellow Christ,* in which women in Breton dress adore the crucified Jesus; *La Belle Angèle,* which was to be bought by Degas in 1891 at the auction that Gauguin himself organized to pay for his voyage to Tahiti; or Gauguin's enigmatic and ironic *Self-Portrait,* now in the National Gallery in Washington, in which he placed a saint's aureole over his head, are good examples of this.

In 1890 and 1891 Gauguin alternated his stays in Le Pouldu with his various lodgings in Paris. However, Gauguin was not out of touch with contemporary urban culture. He came out strongly in favor of modern architecture – he stoutly defended the newly-built Eiffel Tower, for example; or he allowed himself to be flattered by some young writers, notably Charles Morice and Albert Aurier. In 1891 the latter published in *Le Mercure de France* the article "Le Symbolisme en peinture", in which he defended Ideaist, Symbolist, Synthetist, subjective, and decorative painting, and spoke of Gauguin as the high priest of this new artistic conception. "This is the art it comforts me to dream about," wrote Aurier, "the art I like to imagine, during those compulsory strolls among the pitiable or infamous artificiality that our industrialized exhibitions are stuffed with. This also is the art which – if I have not misinterpreted the thought behind his art – this artist has sought to bring to our pitiful, rotten country, this great and brilliant artist with a soul that is primitive, even a little savage: Paul Gauguin."

Gauguin also made contacts with several writers who were then very highly regarded in France. Charles Morice introduced him to Stéphane Mallarmé and, through the great Symbolist poet, he met Octave Mirbeau, the prestigious art critic. Gauguin even attended a banquet given by the Symbolists in honor of Jean Moréas, among other occasions of this type.

At all events, in the early years of the eighteen-nineties, the idea began to take shape in Gauguin's head of taking flight once more to mysterious lands, directly to recover the primitivism that would lead him forward along his artistic path.

To this end, taking advantage of his new contacts in the cultural world of Paris, on 22 February 1891 he organized a sale of work in the Hôtel Drouot, on the proceeds of which he intended to fund his next journey to Tahiti. The venture enjoyed the support of, among others, Mallarmé and Mirbeau, who even published an article in *Le Figaro* announcing the forthcoming auction. Gauguin raised nearly ten thousand francs from the sale of thirty paintings, and at once began conscientious preparations for his voyage to Polynesia. In early March he visited Copenhagen to say goodbye to his wife Mette and the children. On 23 March, Mallarmé presided over a banquet at the Café Voltaire in Paris to pay tribute to Gauguin shortly before his departure. It was attended by, among others, painters, sculptors, and writers such as Odilon Redon, Eugène Carrière, Jean Moréas, Charles Morice, Albert Aurier, Rachilde (Marguerite Valette) and her husband, and by Saint-Pol Roux. Mallarmé proposed the first toast in these words: "Gentlemen, first things first: let us drink to the return of Paul Gauguin; and in admiration of this superior consciousness that exiles its talents, so as to strengthen them, far away yet introspectively, at the moment of their bursting forth."

*The engravings of the* Encyclopédie des Voyages *fed his great dreams of travel. Gauguin said that he went away to free himself from the influence of civilization.*

## GAUGUIN IN POLYNESIA

On 1 April 1891 Gauguin embarked on the *L'Océanien* at Marseilles, sailed through the Suez canal, landed in the Seychelles, and in the Australian cities of Adelaide, Melbourne, and Sidney, and finally made a lengthy stay in Nouméa in New Caledonia. Thence he embarked in the warship *La Vira* for the voyage to Papeete, capital of French Polynesia, where he arrived on 9 June, more than two months after leaving Paris. The people of Papeete were startled by his clothing and, in particular, by his long hair. The natives, not without irony, called him *taatavahine*, that is, half man, half woman. Gauguin, seeking to avoid offence, had his hair cut, dressed in the white colonial style, and began to associate with members of the local European community, especially Lieutenant Jénot, who has left us an account of their meeting. Meanwhile, on 13 August 1891 in Paris, Germaine was born, daughter of Gauguin and Juliette Huet, with whom he had had a relationship as model and lover beginning in the autumn of 1890 during his last stay in Paris.

In autumn 1891, briefly accompanied by Titi, an Anglo-Tahitian girl, he moved to Mataiea, a little village to the south of the capital. There he began to make notes for future paintings, according to his letters to Daniel de Monfreid, his best contact in Europe in those years. More important still, he began to live a primitive, almost savage, life; the life he had been seeking for years. A case in point was the warning he received from the authorities for bathing naked on the beaches of Mataiea, offending public decency. Gauguin found himself in an exceptional setting, highly favorable to his lethargic creativity, which he described thus to his wife Mette: "There is nothing, not even the cry of a bird to break the silence. Now and again there falls a big dry leaf, but without making the slightest noise. It is a kind of caressing of the spirit. The natives often walk by at night, but bare-footed and silent. Always this silence. Now I understand why these people can spend hours or even days sitting down, without saying a word, looking at the sky melancholically. I feel imbued by it all." Gauguin felt himself invaded by this silence, by a profound feeling of peace, of tranquillity, of the sort that the Greeks called ataraxia. This sensation was reinforced by the presence of Teha'amana, a young native girl with whom he lived during his stay in a little cabin in Mataiea. His new wife, as he himself called her in *Noa Noa*, the account he wrote of his first journey to Tahiti, appears in numerous pictures of this period, the incarnation of a sort of ideal primitive woman. By December 1891 Gauguin had painted some twenty canvases, some of which are among his most important contribution to modern western art: *The Meal, Vahine no te Tiare, Ia orana Maria, Te tiare farani* and *Tahitian Women*, to mention but a few.

However, the peace and tranquillity of Mataiea were coming to an end. Gauguin began vomiting blood and had to be admitted to hospital in Papeete; then, after his recovery, he was once again in financial difficulties. At the end of March he informed his friend Paul Sérusier that he wanted to return to France, and a few weeks later he wrote to Mette to inform her that he had recently painted thirty-eight pictures and that he was looking for financial help to return. Gauguin was in a painter's

paradise; later he declared that the landscape dazzled him and blinded him, but he must have felt lonely and absolutely desolate as a person. For a year Gauguin was considering abandoning painting and becoming an inspector of art teaching in Paris. He told Mette of this in February 1893. Finally, on 4 June 1893 he obtained a passage thanks to the French Interior Ministry, which paid the third-class fare. Gauguin said goodbye to Teha'amana, with whom he had shared his stay in Tahiti, first in Mataiea and in the last months in Papeete. In spite of his depression, he had produced a lot of important work. He had been through one of the most significant periods of his evolution as a painter, and presumably with regret, he set out for France once more.

The return journey was once again a difficult one. The *Duchaffault*, in which he had sailed from Tahiti on 4 June, landed him in New Caledonia two weeks later, and he could not continue his voyage until 16 July, when he boarded the *Armand Béhic* for the passage to Marseilles. The vessel docked on 30 August 1893 and Gauguin immediately took the train to Paris with the two hundred and fifty francs that Paul Sérusier had sent him. Thus, at the age of forty-five, he began to live in France again, where he was to remain for almost two years before returning to Polynesia. During this time, he re-established contact with Parisian cultural circles and had the good fortune to inherit half the estate of his uncle Isidore Gauguin, who died in early September 1893.

To take financial advantage of his stay in Tahiti, Gauguin, together with Charles Morice, wrote *Noa Noa*, in which he set out to explain the transformation his painting had undergone. At the same time, Gauguin prepared, with the aid of Degas, Daniel de Monfreid, and Morice, an exhibition of forty-one of the canvases he had painted in Tahiti, plus three from his Breton period and other items. The exhibition, which opened on 10 November 1893 in the Durand-Ruel family's gallery, aroused great curiosity and the criticism from literary circles was more favorable than that from strictly artistic ones. However, Gauguin declared himself to be pleased: "The most important thing for me is that my exhibition has been a great artistic success, and has aroused both anger and jealousy. The press has treated me as they have never treated anyone before, that is, reasonably and with praise." However, from the financial point of view the exhibition was a relative failure; Gauguin sold only eleven paintings, two of which were bought by his friend Degas. His Primitivist painting had still not been accepted. The Musée du Luxembourg, for example, declined Gauguin's donation of *Ia orana Maria*.

*In 1894, Gauguin wrote* Noa Noa *in Paris from notes he had taken in Tahiti. He illustrated them with numerous wood engravings, such as this* Navenave Fenua *(delicious earth).*

In January 1894 he set up his studio in the Rue Vercingétorix. He decorated the walls with Tahitian colors and shapes and hung some original works by Cézanne and Van Gogh that he still had in his collection. At this time he began to live with Annah, a thirteen-year-old Javan girl who also acted as a model until, in late summer or early autumn while Gauguin was in Pont-Aven, she disappeared after having stripped the Paris studio. During the summer in Pont-Aven, Gauguin was attacked by some sailors, with the result that one leg was immobilized and caused severe pain, which the painter tried to mitigate with morphine and alcohol.

His contacts with the French Symbolists, especially Mallarmé, continued; they even arranged several events in his honor. In Pont-Aven he also met Alfred Jarry, who dedicated three poems to him, and August Strindberg, whom he asked for a preface to the catalogue for the next sale of his work; the writer declined to do so, in an exchange of letters that has become famous. Strindberg, along with other members of the cultural milieu, used to attend conversational evenings in Gauguin's studio in Rue Vercingétorix. But in spite of all this activity, Gauguin wrote a letter in September 1894 to Monfreid, informing him that he had decided to leave Europe for good and go to live permanently in Polynesia: "I have taken a firm decision: to go to Polynesia forever. I shall return to Paris in December simply to sell up all my bits and pieces for whatever they will fetch. If I succeed, I shall then leave immediately." The process as recorded by Gauguin in 1894 was a long one, beset by vicissitudes and financial difficulties, since the auction of his work at the Hôtel Drouot on 18 February 1895 brought him only two thousand two hundred francs. His decision was a firm one, however, and on 28 June 1895, Paul Gauguin left Paris for the last time.

On 3 July 1895 he sailed from Marseilles on board the steamer *L'Australien*. While ashore in Auckland, New Zealand he studied the Maori collection in the recently-opened Ethnology Museum. Finally, he reached Papeete on 9 September 1895. At first, and in spite of the fact that he found Tahiti disappointing because of the amount of westernization that had taken place on the island, he went to live in Punaauia, on the west coast, near Papeete. There, he rented some land and built a *fari*, a traditional cabin constructed of

*In 1894 Gauguin painted this* Self-Portrait with Hat *(Musée d'Orsay, Paris) at his Montparnasse studio. All the decoration is reminiscent of Tahiti: the walls painted in bright colors, the multicolored fabrics, the hanging canvases he had painted on the islands which his friends came to admire.*

bamboo and palm leaves. Since Teha'amana, his former Tahitian companion, had been married, he found a new model in the person of Pahura, a fourteen-year-old native girl who became his new lover. However, there soon began a period that was particularly sorrowful for him; in June 1896 he was admitted for the first time to the hospital in Papeete, desperately poor and tormented by pain. Also, Pahura gave birth to a child that died shortly afterwards. The financial situation improved slightly over the next few months thanks to the sums he received from the sale of his pictures in Europe, but his health grew worse. In January 1897, he was admitted to hospital again. And shortly later he received news, by way of a "short and brutal" letter from his wife, of the death of his daughter Aline from pneumonia. He was overwhelmed by sadness, by grief. In summer 1897 his health grew still worse; in addition to the pains in his leg he suffered from an eye infection, the aftermath of an old syphilis infection, skin eruptions that the natives fearfully attributed to leprosy, and finally a heart condition that made him think in October that death was near, and that in December obliged him to enter hospital again. The outlook was frankly desperate. In this time of doubt, Gauguin tried to commit suicide with arsenic, but also began work on his monumental canvas, *Where do we come from? What are we? Where are we going to?*, which has the ring of a testament for posterity.

*Journeys in search of the primitive and savage were a constant urge of Gauguin's, leading him to the island of Taboga in Panama, Martinique, Tahiti, and the Marquesas, where he died. A month before his death he wrote to Morice, "Solitude is not to be recommended to everyone, because you have to be very strong to bear it and to act alone."*

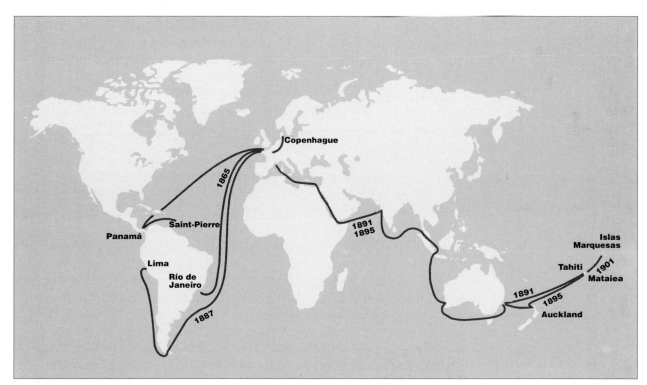

The fact is that the paintings carried out in these first few months back in Tahiti do not reflect this tension and hopelessness. Quite the contrary; Gauguin painted pictures full of color and balance and sketched some fleeting but incredibly intense spiritual portrayals of island life. In 1898 and 1899 he painted *The White Horse, The Idol, Nevermore, Vairumati,* and many other pieces that encapsulate the idea of art that

*Basalt tiki statue in Raivavaé, French Polynesia, Papara. Gauguin was fascinated by Tahitian mythology, which he combined in his work with Western culture.*

Gauguin espoused at that time. "Here, close to my cabin, in complete silence, I dream of violent harmonies whose natural perfumes intoxicate me. A delight extracted from who knows what sacred horror that I perceive in the present. Figures of animals, rigid like statues: there is something ancient, august, religious in the rhythm of their attitude, in their strange stillness."

All this time his life was still plagued with doubt and complications. In April 1899 his companion Pahura bore him another child, whom he called Émile, but he had only a hundred francs left from the money he had received from Paris from the sale of some of his pictures. Disappointed, Gauguin stopped painting. His health grew weaker, and he began to work for the satirical publication *Les Guêpes* in Papeete, of which he later became editor-in-chief. Later, he founded his own paper, *Le Sourire*, which he wrote, illustrated, and printed himself. In *Les Guêpes* Gauguin carried on a campaign against the Protestant Party and Governor Gallet. Also with this paper, for which he worked intensely until August 1901, and which brought him a regular income, he campaigned against the Chinese immigrants. On 23 September 1900 he made a speech on behalf of the Catholic Party in Papeete in which he strongly attacked "this yellow stain that befouls our national flag."

In September 1901, he left Tahiti for Hiva Oa, the most civilized island of the Marquesas archipelago, and the one where the capital, Atuona, stands. The decision to move was not taken rashly; he had reached an arrangement with the gallery owner Ambroise Vollard under which Gauguin would receive a monthly salary for his creative work. Thus, after a long stay in hospital earlier in the year and after selling his few possessions in Tahiti, he embraced this new change in his life with an enthusiasm similar to that which he had shown in previous eras: "With new and wild materials, I am going to make beautiful things. My imagination was beginning to run cold here..." On arrival on the island, he was enthusiastically received, not however, because of his painting, but – paradox of paradoxes in the life of Gauguin – because of is campaigning articles in *Les Guêpes*. Very soon, Gauguin bought some land from Bishop Martin and built a cabin which he christened "Maison du Jouir". In November 1901 he moved into his new home, accompanied by a cook, two maids, a dog, and a cat. This group was soon joined by Vaeoho Marie-Rose, his new model and companion, but she did not stay long; in mid-August she returned to her parents pregnant. In September she gave birth to a baby daughter, but she and Gauguin were not to live together again.

Meanwhile, in this last period of his life, Gauguin was painting again and produced works of tremendous pictorial content. From Hiva Oa he regularly sent canvases to Europe, where Vollard took care of their exhibition and sale. He was also writing. He concentrated on the volume of memoirs *Avant et après*, which was not to be published

until 1923, after the painter's death. He also completed the manuscript *L'Esprit moderne et le catholicisme*, a reflection on the Gospels and an attack on the contemporary church. His outspoken attitude to the church, the governor, and the local police led to problems with the law, to the extent that in April 1903 he was condemned to a month in jail and a fine of five hundred francs. The sentence, however, could never be carried out; Paul Gauguin died on 8 May 1903 at his home in Hiva Oa. Far, far away; almost at the antipodes of Paris, and far closer to Lima, Peru, where Gauguin had spent his early childhood in close contact with the primitive, close to the atavism that was to attract him for the rest of his life. After his death, his reputation underwent a slow but decisive recovery. Thus, as so often in the history of modern art, what was denied to the artist in his lifetime was restored to him after his death. Nonetheless, Gauguin himself, that "savage in spite of myself," as he called himself on one occasion, seemed to intuit an absolute truth: "I am convinced I have been right about art... and even if my work does not survive, there will always remain the memory of an artist who liberated painting."

*On the island of Hiva Oa, Gauguin built a hut which he baptised* Maison du Jouir. *To provoke the Catholic missionaries who criticized his sexual behavior, on two of the sculpted lintels which frame the front door he wrote, "Be mysterious" and "Love and you will be happy".*

**STILL LIFE WITH MANDOLIN,** 1885
Oil on canvas, 64 x 53 cm
*Musée d'Orsay, Paris*

## STILL LIFE WITH MANDOLIN

In 1885, after his early artistic activities under the Impressionist banner, Gauguin painted this picture, in which we may perceive a desire to progress to a more personal style. In appearance, it is a less intense work than some of Gauguin's more typical canvases. However, it was just at this time that he told his painter friend Camille Pissarro that he was going through an absolutely despairing period of his life. "The only thing that keeps me going is painting," wrote Gauguin. So, at a time of fierce emotional tensions and depression, the only

light Gauguin saw at the end of the tunnel was his work as a painter. This view of painting as obsession can be discerned in the painting's circular composition, in the play of contrasts and in the use of color. The objects in the center of the composition are rounded, curved, like the plate on the left, the mandolin, the vase, and the table-mat. All of them are on the table, which also seems to be round. This roundness is emphasized by the contrast with the background of the picture, the straightness of the wall behind, and the picture hanging on it, which can be seen to be a landscape with evident Impressionist characteristics, a suggestive play of

a painting within the painting. The use of color, too, evinces Gauguin's considerable mastery of the painter's craft. The blue of the wall on the right harmonizes with the intense hues of the vase. Also, the greens in the Impressionist landscape enter into a dialogue with the variegated hues of the spray of flowers on the table. The treatment of *Still Life with Mandolin* shows that Gauguin was already a painter with a mastery of the medium and one who felt a need to express his feelings and concerns. Thus, the mandolin, the instrument he was to take with him on his eventual journey to Tahiti, can be seen as a symbol of the harmony that Gauguin could find only in his painting, and not in his personal life.

**WASHERWOMEN IN
PONT-AVEN,** 1886
Oil on canvas, 71 x 90 cm
*Musée d'Orsay, Paris*

**WASHERWOMEN IN
PONT-AVEN**

It was the turmoil of his
private life that led
Gauguin to Brittany, in
search of the inner peace
that would enable him to
paint. However, the first
works he painted that
summer in Pont-Aven still
evince an Impressionist
technique and conception.
In this landscape painted
in 1886, for example,
Gauguin composed a
scene that is perfectly in
tune with Impressionist

ideals. It is a rustic study
of the Breton countryside,
painted with the
characteristic narrow,
juxtaposed brushstrokes
favored by the
Impressionists, who then
formed the avant-garde.
These were rendered with
consummate artistic skill.
Attention should perhaps
be drawn to one detail:
the presence of the
Breton women, the
washerwomen of the title,
in Gauguin's painting.
These women, in their
age-old, primitive

traditional dress, with the distinctive white wimples, were to have a significant role in the artist's later work. They appear, for example, in many of the pictures that Gauguin painted between his first visit to Pont-Aven in summer 1886 and his return and intermittent presence there in early 1888. In the meantime, something else had happened that was to be highly significant in Gauguin's life: his journey to Martinique, where he made direct, passionate contact with primitive, wild, and, for him, virgin surroundings.

**THE VISION OF THE SERMON OR JACOB WRESTLING WITH THE ANGEL,** 1888
Oil on canvas, 73 x 92 cm
*National Gallery of Scotland, Edinburgh*

**THE VISION OF THE SERMON OR JACOB WRESTLING WITH THE ANGEL**

"I have just painted a religious picture that is very badly done, but it was interesting to do and I like it. I wanted to give it to the church in Pont-Aven. Naturally, they don't want it." Gauguin wrote thus to Vincent Van Gogh in late September 1888. He was referring to this painting. The reasons for the church's refusal seem obvious. In fact, the theme of the picture is religious – specifically it is inspired by a passage from Genesis – but Gauguin's execution reveals a splendid intuition of what is the artifice in painting, and with a valor that was exceptional for the time. In the lower left corner of the picture he has placed a group of Breton women, praying with eyes closed and in a meditative posture. In the upper right corner, by contrast, Gauguin shows the spectator what the women can see in their mind's eye: Jacob is wrestling

through the night with the mysterious angel, in a struggle that can be interpreted as the struggle of man against the devil or against himself.

In this painting, Gauguin achieved one of the finest examples of European pictorial symbolism, and departed from typically Impressionist themes, although he was to return to them from time to time. Here, the vision of the landscape is anti-naturalistic; the crucial aspect is the representation, the presentation, of a mental image. The way of achieving this representation is equally extraordinary. Firstly, because of the "staging", the almost cinematographic perception of space *avant-la-lettre*. The women in the foreground, of whom we see only their backs and their wimples, would have been unthinkable in the conventional painting of the period, and even afterwards. Secondly, because of the use of color. The concept of Synthetism takes shape for the first time in Gauguin's painting in an organic way. Thus, the landscape and the figures are represented by means of large, strictly-delimited areas of color, which are even bounded by a narrow black line, instead of the undifferentiated, narrow, contiguous brush-strokes of Impressionism.

## STILL LIFE WITH FRUIT

In the course of 1888, Gauguin and a number of other painters who were staying in Brittany, one of whom was Émile Bernard, devised the idea of Synthetist painting. It was Gauguin who championed the proposal, and it was he who was to develop it. However, not all the work in this period of the painter of the *Vision of the Sermon* is so forcefully conceived. We turn now to two still lifes in which we shall see that in art changes do not usually happen suddenly, but rather are the result of a gradual evolution. An example of this is this picture, painted in summer 1888. It is a still life which, like others of the same period, such as *Still Life with Three*

**STILL LIFE WITH FRUIT,** 1888
Oil on canvas, 43 x 58 cm
*Pushkin Museum, Moscow*

*Puppies,* seeks different solutions for the spatial disposition of the objects represented on the canvas. Once again then, Gauguin is pursuing his own search for the secrets of pictorial representation. However, here he has introduced a dramatic element that is impossible to ignore – the face in the upper left-hand corner. It is a face which, on the one hand, breaks with the typical scheme of still lifes, since the spectator's gaze is drawn to this strange character, treated with the same technique as the inanimate objects in the picture. On the other, the inclusion of this head leaning on the knuckles may be an example of the symbolism that Gauguin sought in his painting.

Hence, some critics have seen in this presumably feminine face, the incarnation of temptation by fruit and the fateful destiny of the human condition. It is no coincidence that this same face appears in a later painting entitled *Human Misery* or *The Wine-Harvest in Arles*.

**WASHERWOMEN AND
GOAT,** 1888
Oil on canvas, 73 x 92
*Museo de Bellas Artes y de Arte
Moderno, Bilbao*

## WASHERWOMEN AND GOAT

Gauguin travelled to
Arles in 1888 and stayed
there for scarcely two
months in the house of
Vincent Van Gogh. In
spite of the shortness of
his stay, Gauguin was
quite close to the strong
and complex personality
of the man who was his
colleague and in spite of
everything his friend, as
well as to the special
character of the Provençal
countryside. While he was
in Arles he returned to,
among other subject-
matter, the washer-women
that he had already painted

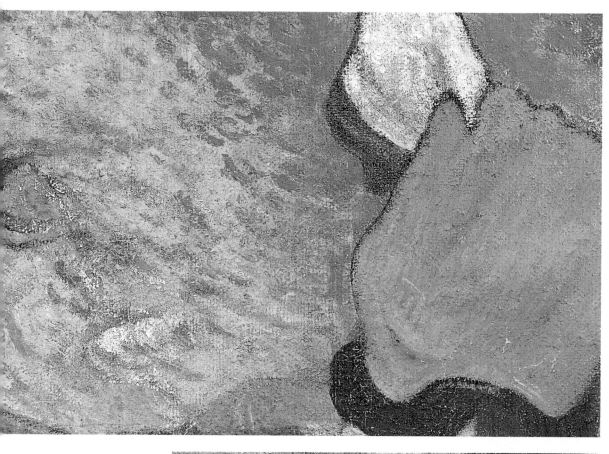

several times. This time the treatment is radically different however. For example, the central theme here is not a general landscape, but a more specific vista of the women of Arles washing clothes. The rest of the landscape is only suggested, and all that can be clearly seen is the goat on the right with its head lowered as though eating. The landscape, or rather, the surroundings of the washerwomen is reduced to a few splashes of color. The women themselves are not portrayed as individuals, their psychology cannot be gleaned from these silhouettes; they are merely presented to us. However, Gauguin's technique here is still Impressionistic. Those patches of color have been created by the application of many small, contiguous brushstrokes, which together give the sensation of broad areas of color in the picture. Nonetheless, the way is clear towards another less detailed approach, far from the anecdotal, in which the sweeping application of a long brushstroke forms a substantial part of the artist's creative message.

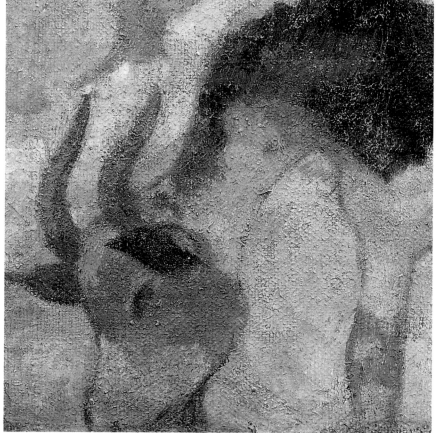

**VIEW OF LES ALYSCAMPS,**
1888
Oil on canvas, 92 x 73 cm
*Musée d'Orsay, Paris*

## VIEW OF LES ALYSCAMPS

The same is to some extent true of this picture, which Gauguin painted during the turbulent period he spent with Van Gogh in Arles. Here however, the process of transformation in his work is more evident. The landscape is defined by the fragmentation of the canvas into several areas of representation, a compositional practice Gauguin was never to abandon. The picture shows the old Roman cemetery of Les Alyscamps, of which at that time there remained "a melancholy avenue of cypresses, lined by rows of empty sarcophaguses, covered with moss and mutilated." In the background can be seen the Romanesque church of Saint-Honorat. It seems to be part of an exercise that he practiced with Van Gogh, since we know of four different versions of the Alyscamps by the Dutch master, some of them executed alongside Gauguin. The colors Gauguin chose were arbitrary, inflamed, and he applied them indiscriminately to a tree with a blue trunk or what one supposes is vegetation in vivid red. The rupture with traditional color is perceptible. The technique perhaps is still miniaturist, but Gauguin has stopped describing what he sees, which is what the Impressionists did. In clear pursuit of his Primitivist ideology, Gauguin was painting what his spirit told him existed, beyond what his senses showed him. Hence, his choice of color was based on an essentially mental process, on a necessarily creative impulse.

### STILL LIFE WITH FAN, 1889
Oil on canvas, 50 x 61 cm
*Musée d'Orsay, Paris*

## STILL LIFE WITH FAN

It seems that Gauguin painted this new still life between 1888 and 1889. A Japanese influence can already be discerned in his earlier work, especially in terms of the spatial organization that is typical of the Orient, and this influence is certainly evident in this picture, which is difficult to date accurately. X-ray examination has shown that it is painted on top of a previous work, of which little or nothing can now be distinguished. However, it has traditionally been dated to 1889, although it could quite easily be rather

earlier.

The fan, which is strongly suggestive of Japan, dominates the composition in tandem with the strange ceramic object on the right, which Gauguin brought from Martinique and which represented the head and horns of what are supposedly two rats. This object brings a good dose of surprise to the picture, since we cannot distinguish the rodents' heads, only what are presumed to be their horns, and the ceramic plays a very different decorative role than that of the fruit and other items in the picture. However, the ceramic must have undergone some modification, since Gauguin had sketched it in one of his notebooks with the rats' heads on either side, and even wrote a letter about it to Émile Schuffenecker. It is interesting to note that both this object and the fan, which also belonged to Gauguin himself, had already appeared in the background of a portrait of Madame Alexander Kohler painted earlier. In fact, the re-use in his work of objects, people, and even the postures of his models was to become habitual throughout his artistic career.

At one time this picture belonged to Prince Matsukata of Japan, who acquired it in Paris on the advice of Léonce Bénédite, who was the curator of the Musée du Luxembourg. Finally, however, the work returned to France as part of Japanese reparations after the Second World War.

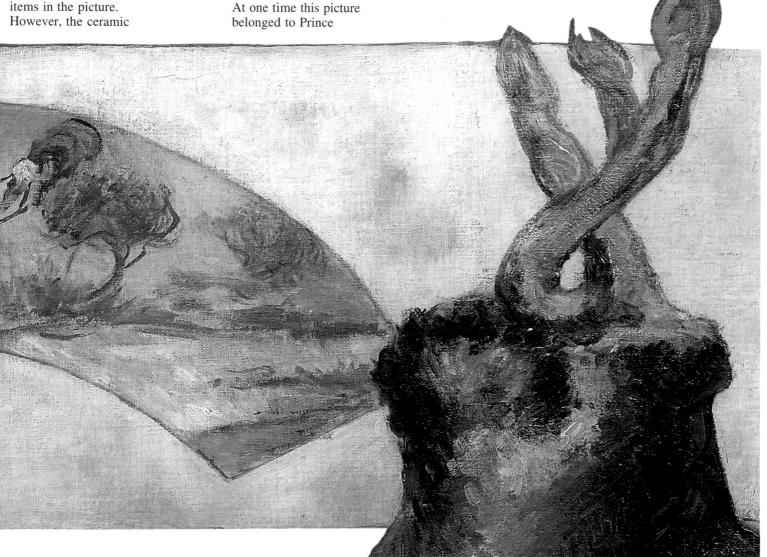

**THE SCHUFFENECKER FAMILY,** 1889
Oil on canvas, 73 x 92 cm
*Musée d'Orsay, Paris*

## THE SCHUFFENECKER FAMILY

In January 1889 Gauguin began work on a surprising picture. It is a group portrait, an unusual subject for him, and furthermore it is satirical in tone, something that is also unusual in his work. This is a portrait of the family with whom Gauguin was staying at the time in Paris. In fact, Émile Schuffenecker was an old friend with whom Gauguin had been quite intimate. But Gauguin's treatment of the couple does not seem to reflect any gratitude on his part; rather it seeks to reflect ugly psychological traits as perceived by the artist. Hence, Madame Schuffenecker gives an impression of deviousness, of bitterness,

ostentatiously showing us
her wedding ring. Perhaps
this is a vengeful joke on
Gauguin's part inspired by
the repeated refusals of his
friend's wife to accept
his amorous proposals.
On other occasions,
Gauguin showed Madame
Schuffenecker in ceramic
works in which he always
included the attribute of a
serpent, the symbol of
temptation.
Plastically, Madame
Schuffenecker is treated
with a disproportionately
large volume,
intentionally so, in
comparison to the
background, no doubt in
search of a certain comic
effect. Her husband, with
his easel beside him, is no
better off; he nas adopted
a comic stance, he is
looking admiringly, but

somewhat stupidly, at his
wife, like a servant in an
operetta. Only the two
little girls, who form one
corner of the central
triangle of the
composition along with
their inflated mother,
seem to be kindly
regarded by the artist.
Also, from the purely
pictorial point of view,
the red of their clothes
matches the reddish
background of the
Japanese print hanging
on the wall of the room
to the right of the
composition.

**LA BELLE ANGÈLE,** 1889
Oil on canvas, 92 x 73 cm
*Musée d'Orsay, Paris*

**LA BELLE ANGÈLE**

In the summer of 1889, Gauguin went back to live in Brittany. It was there that he painted this picture, one of the best-known of what we might call his European output. It is a portrait of Marie-Angélique Satre, which the subject recalled in an interview given in 1920. Thanks to this we know that it was painted in Pont-Aven, just before Gauguin moved to the neighboring village of Le Pouldu, and that the model's first reaction when the artist showed her the finished picture was, "Quelle horreur !" No doubt expecting a conventional, naturalistic portrait, she was unable to understand what Gauguin meant.

Indeed, Gauguin has not sought to capture the subject's facial features, but to paint a Symbolist picture within which the person takes on an emblematic role (rigid posture, charmless expression, festive dress). A factor that greatly contributes to this is the separation of the human figure from the decorative background by a circular arc that does not fall entirely within the frame of the picture, within which is the figure of Marie-Angélique. This procedure may have been suggested to Gauguin by certain Japanese prints that were then becoming known in France. The Symbolist association is heightened by the inclusion, on the left of the composition, of the anthropomorphic ceramic figure, probably Peruvian, that contrasts with the human; it seems as though the ceramic has more life in it than Angèle, trapped within the curved container that emphasizes her lifeless expression. In a letter to his brother Vincent, Theo Van Gogh defined the work as a good Gauguin, and went on to say, "It is a portrait, arranged on the canvas like the large heads on Japanese crepes; first you see the head and shoulders, then you see the background. It shows a seated Breton woman, with her hands in her lap, dressed in black with a purple apron and white jabot; the background

around the figure is gray, while that of the rest of the picture is a beautiful blue with pink and red flowers. The facial expression and the posture are very well-done. The woman looks a bit like a young cow, but there is something so fresh, and once again so rustic, that is extremely pleasant to look at."

### SOYEZ MYSTÉRIEUSES (BE MYSTERIOUS)

Gauguin travelled to Tahiti for the first time in April 1891. However, his desire to discover new countries and new horizons that would restore to him a spirit of the primitive, the undiscovered, began to make itself felt before this in several works. One such work is this one, executed in September 1890 with an abundantly significant title. It is a piece in carved and painted wood, a medium he had used the previous year for *Soyez amoureuses, vous serez heureuses* (Love and you shall be happy). The primitivism of this work draws no doubt on information about distant countries that was accessible to Gauguin in the Universal Exposition held in Paris in 1889, where furthermore the idea of fleeing to Polynesia must have germinated or indeed taken root.

This work has the added attraction of being an example of the degree of excellence Gauguin achieved in other media, such as ceramics or, as in this case, reliefs in wood. The central theme of the work is inspired by a picture Gauguin himself had painted the year before, *In the Waves* or *Ondine,* whose central figure is repeated here with slight positional variations. Nonetheless, we can discern clear differences in the general treatment: here, the undine has become tribalized and the sea has become enigmatically rough. Also enigmatic are the two faces placed on the diagonal, in opposite

**SOYEZ MYSTÉRIEUSES**
**(BE MYSTERIOUS),** 1890
Painted wood (lime),
73 x 95 x 0.5 cm
*Musée d'Orsay, Paris*

corners of the composition; the one on the right seems to represent the moon, the symbol of seduction *par excellence;* the one on the left, much more mysterious, may represent a Breton girl, somewhat malign if we study her expression. This painted wood relief brings us to the full flood of Gauguin's primitivism; the undine is surrounded by sinuous green reliefs, representing the waves and the spume of the tumultuous sea. It is an archaic and dazzling vision that probably draws on a Japanese painted wood-carving that Gauguin could have seen in the April 1889 number of the magazine *Japon artistique.*

**SELF-PORTRAIT,** 1889
Oil on panel (oak), 79.6 x 51.7 cm
*National Gallery of Art (Chester
Dale Collection), Washington*

## SELF-PORTRAIT

Before leaving for Tahiti, Gauguin was still painting enigmatic works that marked the definitive end of one stage of his career and ushered in the start of another. This painting is split into two areas of intense and absolute color: red and yellow. Here Synthetist ideas reach their maximum expression: two compartments, two large blocks of color, dominate the picture. And, on top of them an effigy-like self-portrait, alongside two apples and with a serpent in the hand, suggesting temptation. With the sly irony we have already encountered in *The Schuffenecker Family,* Gauguin pokes fun at himself, representing himself as a tempter, and even putting a halo over his head, a halo that may be interpreted as a sign of sanctity or as an expression of the profoundest demoniac perversion. Gauguin was about to set forth for the unknown, for a nature and a society in embryo, and hence his ethical concepts must have been ambiguous. Gauguin was saying farewell to the western world as an artistic magus, an initiate of the intellectual plane. His irony does not hide the resentment he feels towards Western society as man, husband, and father, or towards the world of art, that does not understand his radical creativity. Consequently, Gauguin was to seek refuge in the virginal world of French Polynesia.

**TE TIARE FARANI
(FLOWERS OF FRANCE),** 1891
Oil on canvas, 72 x 92 cm
*Pushkin Museum, Moscow*

### TE TIARE FARANI
### (FLOWERS OF FRANCE)

It seems likely that this is one of the first pictures Gauguin painted after reaching Tahiti. At least, it still does not have the features that were to characterize his work in Polynesia, although he was on his way to defining them. The composition is fairly conventional, in the sense that the main motif is a spray of flowers placed on a table. Even the treatment of these flowers has a good deal more to do with the still lifes that Gauguin painted in his Impressionist period than with his more recent Synthetist or Symbolist tendencies. One could go further; critics have often pointed out the points of contact there are between Gauguin's work and that of other artists such as Cézanne or Manet. Or indeed Degas; for example, his *Woman Beside a Vase,* painted in 1865.
Nonetheless,
the background of the painting prefigures what was soon to resolve itself into Gauguin's Tahitian style: several rectangular areas overlapping each other and the faces of some natives who seem to be looking at something outside the picture. The young man on the left, of whom Gauguin made a small sketch in one of his notebooks, is looking directly at the viewer, whereas the young woman is looking sideways, her glance diverging from that of the young man. The artist was still cautious in

capturing his tribal figures. From now on, however, there began in Gauguin's painting a recurrent dialogue between Europe, symbolized here by the vase and, even more so, by the central theme itself, and the primitive world whose influence was to grow stronger and stronger. At this point, it seems Gauguin still had not come to terms with the landscape he had just discovered. He still did not venture, therefore, to capture it in paint and needed to take refuge, as it were, in an interior before he was ready to set out to conquer his surroundings with his painting – a conquest that was about to begin.

**THE MEAL OR THE
BANANAS,** 1891
Oil on canvas, 73 x 92 cm
*Musée d'Orsay, Paris*

**THE MEAL OR THE
BANANAS**

In this painting the role of
the native element is more
decisive, although this is
still not the artist's
primitive painting style.
Here once again, Gauguin
has created a still life
under the gaze of some
native children. But the
process of de-
occidentalization is much
more evident; the items
that are typical of
European still lifes have
been replaced by others,
typical of the life of the
islands. Hence, here for the
first time we find *fei*, those
red bananas that must have
made such an impression
on Gauguin, or the bowl
that the islanders typically
use for cooking fish, or
some wild citrus fruit.
With elongated brush-
strokes, with ever-more
aggressive colors, Gauguin
was still dealing with
themes from the European
artistic tradition, but was
subverting them in a
masterly way through
extraordinary
transformations of the
subject matter or of the

line he used. Furthermore, there are touches of mystery, as we find in the upper right-hand corner of the picture, where we can see an adult figure, seated, casting a long shadow over the yellow ground. We may only speculate as to why Gauguin introduced this figure. Soon, the process of Gauguin's absorption into the new world that surrounded him was to bring extraordinary results; for example, his first religious fable in Polynesia, entitled *Ia orana Maria*.

**TAHITIAN WOMEN OR
ON THE BEACH,** 1891
Oil on canvas, 69 x 91 cm
*Musée d'Orsay, Paris*

**TAHITIAN WOMEN OR
ON THE BEACH**

Gauguin was
overwhelmed by the
sensations of his new
world, sensations of light
and color as well as inner
feelings. In Tahiti Gauguin
found new arguments for
abandoning painting as a
simple reflection of reality
and to turn his plastic
creations into the
revelation of his own
world, half-way between
the subjective and the
objective, as he had
already done in many
works in Europe. In this
canvas painted in 1891,
we can see this tendency.
At first sight, the painting
seems to represent a
bucolic scene, two women
sitting on the beach. But
we immediately realize
that the painting reveals a
state of mind, a very
special calm.
Pictorially, the work
revolves round the
contrast between two
large areas of color. To
Gauguin it was wrong
to represent the beach and
the sea naturalistically
in the hope that this would
transmit a sensation of
pleasure to the viewer.

He opted to transmit this sensation through the opposition of blocks of color applied to nature (the sand, the sea, the horizon, the sky) and especially, to these two women, so corporeal and yet so enigmatic at the same time. They exude the same spiritual stability as the two figures in another work by Gauguin that closely resembles this one, entitled *Parau Api (The News of the Day)*, in which the two girls differ hardly at all from these, apart from the clothing of the one on the right, which is somewhat more striking than in this version. It should be mentioned that in this painting the woman on the left is wearing the same floral cotton garment as the virgin in *Ia orana Maria*, a habitual resource of Gauguin's. He was further to maintain and intensify this pictorial conception in his subsequent work on Tahiti.

**IA ORANA MARIA
(HAIL MARY)**, 1891-1892
Oil on canvas, 113.7 x 87.7 cm
*Metropolitan Museum (Sam A.
Lewisohn bequest), New York*

## IA ORANA MARIA
(HAIL MARY)

In this painting Gauguin
has composed a symbolic
representation, a religious
allegory in which an angel
with yellow wings shows
two Tahitian natives, the
Virgin Mary, and child
Jesus. The curiosity of the
work, however, lies in
the fact that Mary and
Jesus, on the right of the
painting and identifiable
by the haloes around their
heads, are also shown as
natives; the child is naked,
while the Virgin is
wrapped in a red floral
cotton garment. It is a

demystifying treatment of
the two figures; the scene
is in the tropics, wild, far
from the grandiloquence
of Western religious
painting. The Tahitian
women are putting their
hands together in an
attitude of respect, but
without ostentation. Mary
and Jesus too are free
from all trace of the
grandiose; their faces
reflect simply serenity
and peace. The natural
background also
contributes to this
sensation of balance, from
the bunches of bananas
in the lower strip of the
composition – the same
bananas as those that
appear in *The Meal* – to
the arch of blue that can
be discerned in the sky, in
the top left-hand corner.
The harmonious scene has
only one Western
reference, a sort of
allusion to the European
cultural tradition. The
angel, also portrayed as a
native, has a form that

seems to be drawn from Renaissance iconography, specifically from the religious paintings of Botticelli.

At the time Gauguin was in Mataiea, a predominantly Catholic area, and very likely it was the collision between two so different cultural, and even geographical, traditions, that suggested this allegorical composition. In fact it seems that the use of color was to some extent determined by the initial idea of the painting. The yellows, reds, blues, and greens that dominate the chromatic composition seem somewhat more restrained than in other pictures, in which color floods certain areas of the canvas without being conceptually determined. Here, color and form are subservient to, or mixed with the idea and theme of the painting, with remarkable balance.

**MATAMOE. LANDSCAPE WITH PEACOCKS,** 1892
Oil on canvas, 115 x 86 cm
*Pushkin Museum, Moscow*

## MATAMOE. LANDSCAPE WITH PEACOCKS

At other times, the Tahitian landscape provoked an outburst of color from Gauguin. This is the case, for example, with this picture, in which he has allowed the pictorial sensations produced by the atmosphere, light, and ambience of Tahiti to flow on the canvas. Of Tahiti, or more precisely, of Mataiea, since the wooden house we can see in the center of the scene is very probably the one he rented in 1891 in that area of Tahiti. At least, this cabin appears in a mythological work on which Gauguin was working in March of the following year, as well as in several water-colors that Gauguin stuck into the manuscript of his book *Noa Noa*, which show the shack from several angles. His stay in Mataiea made a great impression on him. Gauguin himself was moved when he described the scene: sea on one side, mountains on the other. In his book *Noa Noa*, he confesses that at first the spectrum of light and color that he found in Mataiea blinded his European eyes. Or perhaps more precisely, his European painter's eyes. This vision of the place is no doubt artificial, even rather romantic, but Gauguin was fully aware that painting is precisely this – artifice. In this play of illusion, he employs some very tall trees, some very bright colors, and forming a substantial part of the landscape, those majestic, sublime peacocks. A woodcutter on the right, and some figures on the track leading to the cabin complete the composition. In general, with this canvas we have come to exciting painting, where the sinuosities of form and the brightness of colors are played off with amazing artistic voluptuousness, impenetrable and disturbing.

**AREAREA
(AMUSEMENT), 1892**
Oil on canvas, 75 x 94 cm
*Musée d'Orsay, Paris*

### AREAREA (AMUSEMENT)

By 1892 when he painted this picture, during his second year in Tahiti, Gauguin had definitively abandoned any Impressionist influence. This process was already under way in the pictures painted in Pont-Aven, in Brittany. But here it has

gone so far that no trace remains of what, to a large extent, still characterized contemporary Western art; among other things, the little juxtaposed brushstrokes that are so typical of Impressionism. Gauguin has definitively simplified the shapes, has synthesized the representation of the landscape in large areas of color that succeed one another, creating a world without volume, without relief. To some extent, Gauguin was going back to the representation of the world as expressed in

European painting before the systematization of perspective in the Middle Ages. The canvas is divided into bands in which various motifs or scenes are placed simultaneously without there being a direct relationship between them. With an extraordinary plastic capacity, with a sublime poetical suggestiveness, it is only the color that is capable of uniting these motifs or scenes.

The subject matter of this painting consists of scenes of Polynesian daily life and tribal ritual. Through his Tahitian period Gauguin idealized the native figures and the tropical surroundings somewhat. Hence we find in several works of this period, as we have already seen, seated women in peaceful attitudes, symbolizing the harmony of the primitive world. In *Arearea* itself, to this paradisiacal world there is added a bucolic vision of figures and scenery. Music once more figures in Gauguin's painting, in the form of a Tahitian flautist absorbed in her music, seated under a tree, as a sign of calm, of inward peace. Far off, a group of dancers perform fervently before a monumental idol, overflowing with an intense spiritualization of the primitive.

## TAHITIAN PASTORALS

This pictorial apotheosis was to have its continuation in this painting, which in a letter to Daniel de Monfreid written in December 1892, Gauguin himself described as one of the best of his recent works. In fact, since it was nearly New Year, and to symbolize the start of a new phase, he dated the canvas 1893. "This time I have made an exception and given it a French title, *Pastorales tahitiennes*," wrote Gauguin, "because I was unable to find the equivalent in Tahitian. I do not know why, but while I was using pure Veronese green and vermilion, I thought it was an old Dutch painting or an old tapestry. Why can this be? Furthermore, the colors of all my paintings seem dull: I think this must be because

**TAHITIAN PASTORALS,** 1892
Oil on canvas, 87.5 x 13.7 cm
*The Hermitage Museum,
St. Petersburg*

I have none of my old canvases with me, nor any art school picture to serve as a point of reference for comparison. What a memory! I am forgetting everything!" Gauguin thought this picture was reminiscent of Dutch painting. Nonetheless, it is one of the peaks of the artist's Polynesian work. The blocks of color are distributed in a suggestive harmony, very considered in spite of the fact that the artist knew full well that color choices as brave as that of the red dog on the foreground would provoke ridicule, if not anger. The arrangement is masterly; once again we have a native women sitting playing the flute and, a little closer to the center, a pretty girl seems surprised at something that is happening outside the picture. Beside the dog, there is the enigmatic element that is so often found in Gauguin's paradisiacal work; in this case, it is some sort of vessel that seems to contain a deliberately ill-defined figure.

**BRETON VILLAGE UNDER THE SNOW,** 1894
Oil on canvas, 62 x 87 cm
*Musée d'Orsay, Paris*

## BRETON VILLAGE UNDER THE SNOW

Gauguin ended his first period in Polynesia in 1893 and returned to France in September of that year. During his short stay there, before returning to his primitive world in June 1895, he stayed for a time in Brittany. Places in Brittany such as Pont-Aven or Le Pouldu became his domestic refuge, the most pleasant substitute in Europe for the distant lands from which he had just returned. In this period, he made some paintings on the basis of notes taken in Tahiti, in which, with Annah the Javanese as his principal model, the landscape of the South Pacific persists. Or ceramics; in 1894 he sculpted *Oviri* (*Wild*), which shows a native girl in a fiery attitude. But he also once again painted pictures of his beloved Breton countryside and people. Hence, in 1894 we find a canvas like this in which it seems that, briefly, Gauguin has become once more an Impressionist painter. Both in this picture and

another painted the same year with similar subject-matter, *Paris under the Snow*, we find some characteristics that are typical of Impressionism that Gauguin knew so well. For example, we discern a simplicity in the composition, in which the artist's point of view is a conventional one as is the structure. Only the coloring and the brush-work are at odds with that Impressionist past. *Breton Village under the Snow* is invaded by white, a color which is scarcely found in the Tahitian works. Only the little contrasts of the buildings of the village oppose themselves to this white blanket. However, the brushwork, although not as extended as in certain earlier works, bears no resemblance to the little brushstrokes of the Impressionism of Gauguin's early career.

**TWO BRETON PEASANTS,** 1894
Oil on canvas, 66 x 92 cm
*Musée d'Orsay, Paris*

## TWO BRETON PEASANTS

In fact, in this period Gauguin had not in the least abandoned his particular way of understanding color. This is shown by canvases such as *The Moulin David in Pont-Aven* or the one we are dealing with here, both painted in 1894. Here, Gauguin returns once again to the Breton countryside. Importantly though, he has placed the two Breton women prominently, once again dressed in peasant clothes and with wimples on their heads. However, their faces are rather different, much more primitive, perhaps suggesting Polynesia. In fact, Gauguin has ritualized his Breton peasant women, or more precisely, he has dressed a Tahitian native woman in the attire typical of that part of France. The schematization of the faces of the women demonstrates this. The landscape that fills the upper part of the composition could, taken on its own, be confused with the leafy natural backgrounds that structure his Tahitian work. These fragments contrast with the country house in the

background, or with the bucolic scenes on the left of the picture. It is only the path on which the women are standing, which crosses the surface of the painting diagonally, that gives the composition unity. Hence, the dialogue between the West and the primitive world once more appears splendidly in Gauguin's work. But this time the allusion is prompted by the longing Gauguin was beginning to feel for his tropical landscapes and the peace and equanimity of the people of those lands. In the end, this dialogue was to proceed without a solution of continuity. It was to occur again during Gauguin's second and definitive stay in Polynesia, first in Tahiti, and finally in the Marquesas. This is not the great, indomitable painting of the Gauguin of Tahiti, but it begins to suggest his definitive course as a painter of the primitive.

**OVIRI (WILD),** 1894
Glazed ceramic, 75 x 19 x 27 cm
*Musée d'Orsay, Paris*

## OVIRI (WILD)

In late 1894 Gauguin
returned to ceramics in
Ernest Chaplet's work-
shop, where he produced
two items: *Primitive Mask*
in plaster, and *Oviri* in
earthenware. The latter
work is specially
noteworthy; first of all
because of its polished
execution, with which
Gauguin achieved a
"sculpture in ceramics",
as he himself described
the piece. Secondly,
because of the influence
the work was eventually
to have on the future of
contemporary painting.
*Oviri* was exhibited at the

autumn Salon in 1906 and it seems highly probable that it was one of the sources of inspiration for Pablo Picasso when he painted his landmark work, *Les Demoiselles d'Avignon*.

"Oviri", in Tahitian, means "wild", an adjective that especially pleased Gauguin the man, lively and adventurous, and Gauguin the artist, lover of primitive shapes and the manifestation of enigma. The sculpture shows a woman, wearing a long head-dress, with bulging eyes, and with a bloody wolf at her feet. The piece exudes wildness in its most violent, or more precisely, aggressive form. Gauguin had decided to go back to Polynesia, despairing of the climate he found in European society, and perhaps the expression of finality that the wild woman transpires is in response to this idea of despair and disturbance. Gauguin reflected a similar expressive forcefulness in his engraving *Oviri*, which he based on the body of the woman, "strange figure, cruel enigma," as the artist defined it in a dedication to his friend, the poet Stéphane Mallarmé. The face appears again, with slight variations, in a number of later works, especially *The Idol* of 1898. There, as in *Oviri* itself, it gives the impression that Gauguin was tending to an esoteric art, one that hid a multitude of secrets that Gauguin could only attain through creation.

### TE TAMARI NO ATUA (THE BIRTH OF CHRIST), 1896
Oil on canvas, 96 x 128 cm
*Neue Pinakothek, Munich*

## TE TAMARI NO ATUA (THE BIRTH OF CHRIST)

One of the first pictorial fruits of the contact between Europe and the tropics on Gauguin's arrival for the second time in Tahiti was this picture, painted between 1895 and 1896 and dated in the latter year. Like *Ia orana Maria*, painted during his first stay in Polynesia, this is an example of Gauguin's very personal interpretation of religious painting. Once again, it is divided into two parts: in the upper part, a native woman holds the newly-born Jesus, while another looks on, and on the right, we can see the

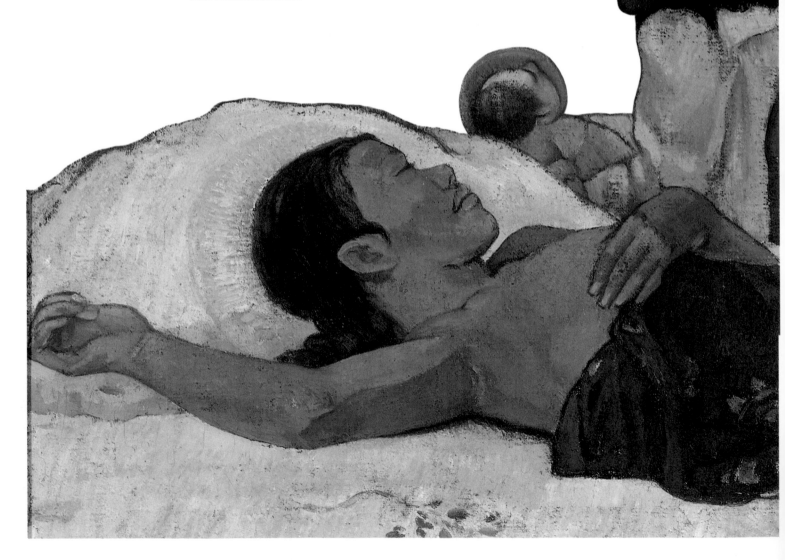

stable. In the lower part, a native girl lies asleep on a bed; presumably this is Mary, who has just given birth, since Gauguin has placed a faint halo around her head. This work is neither more nor less than a new representation of the Nativity, but with the characteristics that we have already found in earlier religious works. Thus, Gauguin has primitivized the whole scene; mother, child, and nurses are Tahitian natives, and are wearing native attire. Only the stable in the upper right-hand corner has clear Western connotations. This is not surprising if we recall that Gauguin's source for the representation of the cattle was a photograph of the picture *Stable Interior* by Octave Tassaert, which had been in the collection of his former tutor Gustave Arosa.

Pictorially this painting is a masterpiece, based on layers of material, on which Gauguin worked in search of a feeling of balance and intensity – chromatic and spiritual intensity. Especially prominent is the intense yellow of the bed on which the mother lies with a white cat asleep at her feet. The main model for this picture was undoubtedly Pahura, the artist's companion at this time, who had given birth to a child in late 1896 that died shortly afterwards. Perhaps the pregnancy of his *vahiné* was a special inspiration to Gauguin to undertake this work, at once religious and primitive.

**WHERE DO WE COME FROM? WHAT ARE WE? WHERE ARE WE GOING TO?,** 1897-1898
Oil on canvas, 139 x 374.5 cm
*Museum of Fine Arts, Boston*

**WHERE DO WE COME FROM? WHAT ARE WE? WHERE ARE WE GOING TO?**

It was in December 1897 that Gauguin painted this monumental work, which is almost four meters long. It was a time of hopelessness and anguish. Gauguin was on the verge of suicide, but first, as he told his friend Daniel de Monfreid, he wanted to paint a large picture he had had in mind for some time, and which he completed in a month, working day and night. It is a sort of fresco whose background is dominated by greens, and, over this a series of human figures, some of them naked with rather orange flesh tones and others in Polynesian native dress. Gauguin was setting out to write his pictorial will, and perhaps because of this, he composed a narrative frieze representing several stages in an individual's evolution: on the left, an old woman, close to death; on the right, a new-born child, and beyond this a dog seems to be observing the sequence intently. Between one figure and another can be seen various Polynesian motifs, scenes, or animals, many of which had appeared in previous paintings or were to be used in later ones. Beside the infant, some young girls sit resting; further to the left, and in the middle ground, some clothed figures seem to be having a deep conversation while another seated figure looks at them reproachfully. In the center, a young girl is picking a fruit; the smoothness of her body speaks of the wondrousness of island life. On the left, in the middle ground, an element

of mystery: an idol with arms raised seems to be rhythmically announcing the next world, the deepest of tribal beliefs. Altogether this is an extraordinarily complex painting, and one in which the plastic treatment is no less vibrant and successful. Begun as an artistic testament, its form and discourse seem open to any interpretation today.

**VAIRUMATI,** 1897
Oil on canvas, 73 x 94 cm
*Musée d'Orsay, Paris*

## VAIRUMATI

Shortly before painting *Where Do We Come from? What Are We? Where Are We Going to?* or at the same time, Gauguin embarked on another work that involves some of the same figures. In fact, the young woman sitting on the floor beside the old woman, and the bird from the lower left-hand corner are the same motifs, caught in the same positions as the ones that form the central theme of *Vairumati*. The young woman's loin-cloth is even folded in the same way as in the other painting. At the time, as Gauguin himself relates in his book *Noa Noa,* he was keenly interested in the ancestral religions of the island and the myths of the natives. This interest led him, according to his memoirs, to discuss the subject with his companion of the time, Teha'amana. The art historian Françoise Cachin, however, puts forward a very plausible theory regarding his main source of information on

these matters, namely the book *Voyages aux îles du Grand Océan* by J. A. Moerenhout. On the basis of this information, Gauguin painted several works on religious or mythical themes, such as *Te aa no areois (The Seed of the Ariois, Manao Tupapau (The Spirit of the Dead is Watching)* or *Vairumati* itself. In this picture, Gauguin draws his inspiration from a native legend and symbolizes it in a painting where the forms are simplified and the pregnant colors enter into a tense, but not altogether inharmonious dialogue. The yellows and reds in the background strike a hard balance with the white of the bird and with the young Tahitians who appear in the foreground and to the rear. The bird, which has a lizard in its claw, and the yellow throne, which is decorated with a relief of a Tahitian divinity, are evidence of this reading of native mythology. While, as we have seen, Gauguin introduces enigmatic elements in apparently naturalistic works, on the other hand, in this piece inspired by legend he places a scene from daily life in the form of the young women seated in the right background.

**THE WHITE HORSE,** 1898
Oil on canvas, 140 x 91 cm
*Musée d'Orsay, Paris*

## THE WHITE HORSE

Also in 1898, Gauguin produced more works in an idyllic, perhaps happier, vein. Here once again, Gauguin brings together two cultural traditions in a single painting. On the one hand, the equestrian theme, which is a recurrent one in Western painting; in this respect, he must have been aware of Degas' paintings of horses, since he had had the opportunity to see them and admire them in Europe. On the other hand, Gauguin is trying to capture, with exceptional pictorial richness, the mysticism of the Polynesian cultures, and in particular the tribal beliefs that regarded white horses as sacred, as the holders of supreme revelation. At all events, the execution is exceptional. Once again Gauguin takes total liberty to schematize the landscape in large blocks, delighting in the color and sinuosity of their shapes. The three horses that can be seen are each painted in a different color, and two of them deserve special attention: the red horse, that is reminiscent of the red dogs Gauguin used to paint, and which had caused quite a few gibes at European exhibitions, and, especially, the white horse which is bending its head to drink from a stream. This horse is not altogether white, but rather its body is a synthesis of the colors of its surroundings, like reflections in water. In the lower part of the composition, Gauguin places an exotic flower and some no less foreign leaves. Once again, it is nature itself that is the main protagonist of Gauguin's painting, of his creation.

**THE GREAT BUDDHA,** 1899
Oil on canvas, 134 x 95 cm
*Pushkin Museum, Moscow*

### THE GREAT BUDDHA

This painting, executed in 1899, is very different from the previous one in both composition and choice of subject. Gauguin sets the scene in an interior, in a building, and consequently the freedom of curves is transformed here into a controlled obedience to rectilinearity. The content of this picture is of great interest. We have several levels: one prosaic, in which some naked women, more sensual than ever, look toward the viewer; the other, religious and mythological. For this level, Gauguin once again resorts to the confrontation of, or dialogue between, different cultures. A dark statue of Buddha reminds us of the religions of distant lands. But behind this is counterpoised by a representation of one of the most traditional biblical themes in the history of Western art – the Last Supper. So once again Gauguin turns to mystery, to enigma. While in *Ia orana Maria* or *Te tamari no atua* he primitivizes Catholic religion, here his references are more diffuse. Or perhaps less so; it could be that Gauguin is showing us, according to his own interpretation, two faces of the same phenomenon. At all events, in the upper right-hand corner a door opens to the exterior, perhaps indicating a possible way out, another possible reading of the scene.

## MOTHERHOOD OR WOMEN ON THE SEASHORE

This painting, also dated 1899, is an ambitious work. It is a sort of hymn to beauty and youthful motherhood, painted with a very special touch. The ambiguity of the dark brown of the girls contrasts with the backgrounds and the attributes Gauguin includes, with reddish and orange shades, dark bottle greens or highly-pigmented blues. Gauguin achieves an exceptional chromatic harmony. He described it to his dealer Ambroise Vollard when, in October 1900, he sent it to be sold in Europe along with ten other canvases: "Three figures: squatting woman suckling an infant, in the foreground; black dog, on the right; on the left, standing woman with red dress and basket; behind, woman in green garment holding flowers. Background of blue lagoons, over orange-red sand, and fisherman." About the same time, Gauguin painted a smaller version of the same scene, with slight color variations. At all events, he shows that he is still a painter in his utmost and most intimate essence. He explained that, through lines and colors, and with the pretext of a theme borrowed from life or nature, he wanted to attain symphonies, harmonies, that represented nothing real in the common sense

**MOTHERHOOD OR WOMEN ON THE SEASHORE,** 1899
Oil on canvas, 95.5 x 73.5 cm
*The Hermitage Museum,
St. Petersburg*

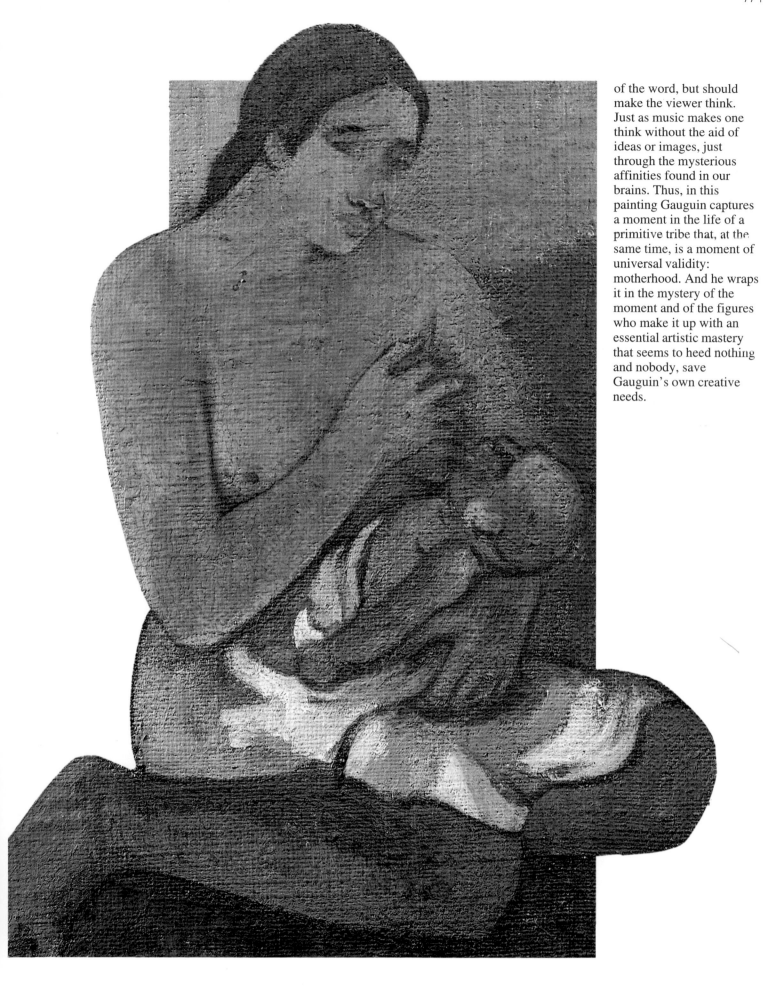

of the word, but should make the viewer think. Just as music makes one think without the aid of ideas or images, just through the mysterious affinities found in our brains. Thus, in this painting Gauguin captures a moment in the life of a primitive tribe that, at the same time, is a moment of universal validity: motherhood. And he wraps it in the mystery of the moment and of the figures who make it up with an essential artistic mastery that seems to heed nothing and nobody, save Gauguin's own creative needs.

**GOLDEN BODIES,** 1901
Oil on canvas, 67 x 76 cm
*Musée d'Orsay, Paris*

## GOLDEN BODIES

The last period of Gauguin's life was spent in the Marquesas archipelago on the island of Hiva Oa. Between September 1901 and his death in 1903 his painting seemed to be rejuvenated by the primitive spirit he found once again in his new home. Tahiti had become over-familiar to him, and now he was inspired to new undertakings, stimulated by the environment of these tropical islands. We can discern this change in a work such as this, in which simplicity reaches its maximum expression. The poetry Gauguin perceived in the natural surroundings is transmitted directly, without apparent mythological or cultural filters.

Gauguin has painted two native girls of Hiva Oa, in an attitude of rest and calm. The colors of the surroundings fade away in order to emphasize the beauty of the naked women. Rarely did Gauguin manage to capture this beauty so seductively, because the central female figure is especially seductive, persuasive. To the primitive, virginal character that Gauguin gave to his earlier female portraits in Polynesia, he now adds a Western touch: the fascination the artist may feel for a naked body and a beautiful face. A fascination he wants to transmit through his painting, through swift, incisive brushstrokes, and one that seems to be beyond mental control. Above all, this formal simplicity and this treatment of color are at the service of pictorial expression in its purest essence.

**THE HORSEMEN OR
THE FORD,** 1901
Oil on canvas, 73 x 92 cm
*Pushkin Museum, Moscow*

## THE HORSEMEN OR THE FORD

We find the same simplicity in this picture, albeit applied to a different subject. In the last years of his life, Gauguin painted several pictures on equestrian themes. We have already seen the great quality of *The White Horse* and the significance for Gauguin of the horse in his work. Some three years later, in 1901, he painted this picture, which has to be seen in relation with others of the same period, especially the later *Horsemen on the Beach,* in which the horsemen have reached the sea and are riding along an immense pink beach. Several artistic traditions merge in this picture; firstly, Degas' equestrian works, with which we know Gauguin was very familiar; secondly, an engraving by Durer, *The Knight, Death, and the Devil,* of which Gauguin had a reproduction; and finally the primitive artistic tradition that Gauguin himself had created during his decade in the tropics.

Some horses are about to ford a river. In the center, a whitish animal, whose body, as in the case of *The White Horse*, reflects other colors from the surroundings. The rider is wearing a pink hood on his head and his aquiline features are reminiscent of Gauguin himself. Behind, on a black horse, comes a native rider who, with a raised arm, seems to be communicating with a bird flying by. In the background, beyond some trees and some ill-defined vegetation, lies the pink sand of the beach with a native vessel. Finally, beyond the beach and in the upper strip of the composition, the sea, rough and stormy, in contrast to the calm blue waters of the ford in the foreground.

**PRIMITIVE TALES,** 1902
Oil on canvas, 131.5 x 90.5 cm
*Museum Folkwang, Essen*

## PRIMITIVE TALES

This is one of Gauguin's last pictures, painted in 1902, a few months before he died at his home in Hiva Oa. It is not too different in appearance from his earlier work: native women in a peaceful pose, seated, with schematic faces; masterly female nudes. Nonetheless, here Gauguin adds another note to the prolonged cult of the bucolic and peaceful Polynesian culture and landscape that we find in his paintings. The picture seems to reflect Gauguin's sorrow in these last months, the entrenchment of his illnesses and the nostalgia he must have felt so far from Europe. Around this time, Gauguin expressed a wish to return to France; not to stay there, but to recover his health and then to flee again in search of new sources of inspiration. This time, he was thinking of going to Spain in search of new horizons, but this project was to come to nothing. With dramatic pictorial effect, it seems that the artist is deliberately making his primitive scenes darker. The calm surroundings seem threatened by this strange, mysterious figure on the upper left-hand side of the painting. A human figure, albeit with somewhat bestial face and extremities. The face is specially enigmatic and suggestive, with glassy eyes and a rather malign

expression. A face in which once again certain traits of Gauguin himself can be discerned. Altogether, the painting is a very disturbing one, as well as an authentic demonstration of Gauguin's unequalled artistic gifts, searching for new sources of inspiration to which he then gave shape in a variety of artistic languages. Octave Mirbeau, referring to Gauguin's first visit to Tahiti, had defined an artist who encompassed all his searching, all his richness, all his truth: "a man who is fleeing from civilization, willingly seeking forgetfulness and silence the better to feel, the better to hear, the interior voices that are drowned out by the din of our passions and our arguments."

# GAUGUIN

## THE COMPLETE WORKS

## WORKS

**1 • Landscape in Autumn, 1871**
Oil on canvas, 65 x 100 cm
*Private Collection*

**2 • Woodland Scene, 1873**
Oil on canvas, 45 x 31 cm
*Private Collection*

**3 • House in the Countryside, 1874**
Oil on canvas, 26 x 33 cm
*Ny Carlsberg Glyptotek, Copenhagen*

**4 • Portrait of Émile Gauguin, 1875**
Oil on canvas, 28 x 27 cm
*Private Collection*

**5 • The Seine at Iena Bridge, 1875**
Oil on canvas, 65 x 92.5 cm
*Musée d'Orsay, Paris*

**6 • The Seine Between the Iéna
Bridge and the Grenelle Bridge
(the Cail Factories), 1875**
Oil on canvas, 81 x 116 cm
*Private Collection*

**7 • Wildflowers in a Blue Vase, 1876**
Oil on canvas, 55 x 38 cm
*Annan Collection, New York*

**8 • Claude-Antoine-Charles
Favre, 1877**
Oil on canvas, 45 x 37 cm
*Private Collection*

**9 • Mette Sewing, 1878**
Oil on canvas, 116 x 81 cm
*Bührle Collection, Zurich*

**10 Apple Trees in the Hermitage,
in the Outskirts of Pontoise, 1879**
Oil on canvas, 65 x 100 cm
*Aargauer Kunsthaus, Aarau*

**11 • Market Gardens
in Vaugirard, 1879**
Oil on canvas, 65 x 100 cm
*Smith College Museum of Art,
Northampton (Massachusetts)*

**12 • Bust of Mette, 1880**
Marble, 34 cm
*Courtauld Institute, London*

**13 • Farms, 1880**
Oil on canvas, 81 x 116 cm
*Sam Spiegel Collection, New York*

**14 • Suzanne Sewing
or Nude Study, 1880**
Oil on canvas, 111.4 x 79.5 cm
*Ny Carlsberg Glyptotek, Copenhagen*

**15 • The Singer or Portrait
of Valérie Roumi, 1880**
Mahogany and plaster, polychromed
and gilded, 54 x 51 x 13 cm
*Ny Carlsberg Glyptotek, Copenhagen*

**16 • Lady Strolling or
The Little Parisienne, 1880**
Painted Laurel wood, 25 cm
*Warburg Collection*

**17 • Flowers, Still Life,
or The Painter's Home,
Rue Carcel, 1881**
Oil on canvas, 130 x 162 cm
*Nasjonalgalleriet, Oslo*

**18 • Sleeping Child
(The Little Dreamer, Study), 1881**
Oil on canvas, 59.5 x 73.5 cm
*Ordrupgaard Collection, Copenhagen*

**19 • Vase of Flowers
in the Window, 1881**
Oil on canvas, 19 x 27 cm
*Musée des Beaux-Arts, Rennes*

**20 • Still Life with Oranges, 1881**
Oil on canvas, 33 x 46 cm
*Musée des Beaux-Arts, Rennes*

**21 • Snow Scene, Rue Carcel, 1882**
Oil on canvas, 60 x 50 cm
*Ny Carlsberg Glyptotek, Copenhagen*

**22 • The Sculptor Aubé
and His Son, 1882**
Pastel on paper, 53.8 x 72.8 cm
*Musée du Petit Palais, Paris*

**23 • A Street in Osny, 1883**
Oil on canvas, 76 x 101 cm
*Ny Carlsberg Glyptotek, Copenhagen*

**24 • Snow Scene, 1883**
Oil on canvas, 60 x 50 cm
*Neil A. Mc Connell Collection*

## WORKS

**25 • Sleeping Child, 1884**
Oil on canvas, 46 x 55.5 cm
*Josefowitz Collection, Lausanne*

**26 • Man's Portrait (Philipsen?), 1884**
Oil on canvas, 65 x 45 cm
*Jaffé Collection, New York*

**27 • Mette Gauguin
in Evening Dress, 1884**
Oil on canvas, 65 x 54 cm
*Nasjonalgalleriet, Oslo*

**28 • Blue Roofs (Rouen), 1884**
Oil on canvas, 74 x 60 cm
*Oskar Reinhart Collection, Winterthur*

**29 • A Forest Floor
in Normandy, 1884**
Oil on canvas, 55 x 46 cm
*Museum of Fine Arts, Boston*

**30 • The Haycart, 1884**
Oil on canvas, 60 x 73 cm
*Wilmers Collection, Brussels*

**31 • The Peonies, 1884**
Oil on canvas, 60 x 73 cm
*Private Collection*

**32 • Town Street, 1884**
Oil on canvas, 55 x 50 cm

**33 • Iridescent Vase, 1884**
Oil on canvas, 55 x 46 cm
*Private Collection*

**34 • Aline and Pola, 1885**
Pastel on paper, 72 x 53.5 cm
*Lloyd Kreeger Collection*

**35 • Self-Portrait, 1885**
Oil on canvas, 65 x 54 cm
*Koerfer Collection, Bern*

**36 • Forest Path, 1885**
Oil on canvas, 81 x 65 cm
*Rijksmuseum Kröller-Müller, Otterlo*

37

38

39

40

41

42

43

44

45

46

47

48

**37 • Cows at the Watering-Place, 1885**
Oil on canvas, 81 x 65 cm
*Galleria Civica d'Arte Moderna,
Milan*

**38 • A Hill in Sèvres, 1885**
Oil on canvas, 55 x 46 cm
*Musée Jacquemard-André, Paris*

**39 • Fan Decorated with a
Portrait of Clovis and Motifs
from a Still Life, 1885**
Gouache on fabric, 32.5 x 56.3 cm
*Ivo Pitanguy Collection*

**40 • Still Life with Mandolin, 1885**
Oil on canvas, 64 x 53 cm
*Musée d'Orsay, Paris*

**41 • Women Bathing (Dieppe), 1885**
Oil on canvas, 38 x 46 cm
*National Museum of Western Art,
Tokyo*

**42 • Still Life in an Interior, 1885**
Oil on canvas, 60 x 74 cm
*Private Collection*

**43 • Vases and Fan, 1885**
Oil on canvas, 100 x 65 cm
*Winthrop Collection, New York*

**44 • The Patron's Son, 1886**
Oil on canvas, 53.5 x 54 cm
*Private Collection*

**45 • Clovis, 1886**
Oil on canvas, 56 x 40 cm
*New Jersey Historical Museum,
Newark*

**46 • Parisian Suburb, 1886**
Oil on canvas, 78 x 57 cm
*Weitzenhoffer Collection, Oklahoma*

**47 • The Watering Hole, 1886**
Oil on canvas, 57 x 70 cm
*Fujikawa Gallery, Osaka*

**48 • Drum Decorated with Fruits, 1886**
Oil on leather, 18 cm
*Lucas Collection*

## WORKS

**49 • The Breton Shepherdess, 1886**
Oil on canvas, 60.4 x 73.3 cm
*Laing Art Gallery,*
*Newcastle Upon Tyne*

**50 • The White Tablecloth;**
**Gloanec Pension, 1886**
Oil on wood, 55 x 58 cm
*Astor Collection, London*

**51 • Self-Portrait for Carrière,**
**1886 (?)**
Oil on canvas, 40.5 x 32.5 cm
*National Gallery of Art, Washington*

**52 • Still Life with Profile**
**of Laval, 1886**
Oil on canvas, 46 x 38 cm
*Private Collection*

**53 • Path in the Forest, 1886**
Oil on canvas, 92 x 73 cm
*Private Collection*

**54 • The Suburbs Pont-Aven, 1886**
Oil on canvas, 60 x 73 cm
*Private Collection*

**55 • Bathing in the Port**
**of Pont-Aven, 1886**
Oil on canvas, 82 x 60 cm
*Private Collection*

**56 • Farm in Brittany, 1886**
Oil on canvas, 73.5 x 112 cm
*Private Collection*

**57 • The Mountain Sainte-**
**Marguerite at Pont-Aven, 1886**
Oil on canvas, 60 x 73 cm
*Private Collection*

**58 • Washerwomen in Pont-Aven, 1886**
Oil on canvas, 71 x 90 cm
*Musée d'Orsay, Paris*

**59 • The Champ Derout-Lollichon**
**(Pont-Aven Church), 1886**
Oil on canvas, 73 x 92 cm
*Private Collection*

**60 • The Derout-Lollichon**
**Fields, 1886**
Oil on canvas, 73 x 92 cm
*Wallis Collection, Los Angeles*

61

62

63

64

65

66

67

68

69

70

71

72

**61 • Jardinière Decorated with Motifs from The Breton Shepherdess and The Toilette, 1886-1887**
Stoneware decorated with barbotine, 27 x 40 cm
*Private Collection*

**62 • Rocks by the Sea, 1886**
Oil on canvas, 71 x 92 cm
*Konstmuseum, Göteborg*

**63 • Cows at the Seaside, 1886**
Oil on canvas, 75 x 112 cm
*Private Collection*

**64 • Rocks by the Sea, 1886**
Oil on canvas, 73 x 93 cm
*Private Collection*

**65 • Still Life with Horse's Head, 1886**
Oil on canvas, 49 x 38 cm
*Private Collection*

**66 • Flowers and Foliage, 1886 (?)**
Oil on paper, 20 cm
*Private Collection*

**67 • Vase with Flowers and Gourd, c. 1886-1887**
Oil on canvas, 58 x 72 cm
*Private Collection*

**68 • Four Breton Women, c. 1886-1888**
Oil on canvas, 72 x 91 cm
*Bayerische Staatsgemäldesammlungen, Neue Pinakothek, Munich*

**69 • Two Girls Bathing, 1887**
Oil on canvas, 87.5 x 70 cm
*Museo Nacional de Bellas Artes, Buenos Aires*

**70 • Exotic Fruits and Red Flowers, 1887**
Oil on canvas, 33 x 46 cm
*Private Collection*

**71 • Tropical Vegetation, 1887**
Oil on canvas, 116 x 89 cm
*National Gallery of Scotland, Edinburgh*

**72 • By the Sea I, 1887**
Oil on canvas, 54 x 90 cm
*Ny Carlsberg Glyptotek, Copenhagen*

## WORKS

**73 • By the Sea II, 1887**
Oil on canvas, 46 x 61 cm
*Private Collection*

**74 • The Small Lake, 1887**
Oil on canvas, 90 x 116 cm
*Neue Pinakothek, Munich*

**75 • In the Town, 1887**
Oil on canvas, 73 x 92 cm
*Private Collection*

**76 • Women and Goats
in the Village, 1887**
Oil on canvas, 46 x 71 cm
*Mitchell Collection*

**77 • Near the Cabins, 1887**
Oil on canvas, 90 x 55 cm
*Suita Trading Company, Tokyo*

**78 • On the Banks of
the Small Lake, 1887**
Oil on canvas, 54 x 65 cm
*Van Gogh Museum, Amsterdam*

**79 • Panoramic Landscape, 1887**
Oil on canvas, 60 x 73 cm
*Van Gogh Museum, Amsterdam*

**80 • Under the Mangos;
Fruit Picking, 1887**
Oil on canvas, 89 x 116 cm
*Van Gogh Museum, Amsterdam*

**81 • Conversation in
the Tropics, 1887**
Oil on canvas, 61 x 76 cm
*Private Collection*

**82 • Cabins Under the Trees, 1887**
Oil on canvas, 92 x 72 cm
*Private Collection*

**83 • Palm Trees, 1887**
Oil on canvas, 112 x 87 cm
*Private Collection*

**84 • Martinique Woman
in the Country, 1887**
Oil on canvas, 45 x 50 cm

85

86

87

88

89

90

91

92

93

94

95

96

**85 • Vase Shaped Like the Bust of a Girl; Portrait of Jeanne Schuffenecker, 1887-1888**
Unglazed stoneware, 19 cm
*Private Collection*

**86 • Snow Scene, 1888**
Oil on canvas, 73 x 92 cm
*Konstmuseum, Göteborg*

**87 • Conversation, 1888**
Oil on canvas, 92 x 73 cm
*Musées royaux d'Art et d'histoire, Brussels*

**88 • First Flowers; Brittany, 1888**
Oil on canvas, 70 x 92 cm
*Kunsthaus, Zurich*

**89 • Young Breton Shepherd, 1888**
Oil on canvas, 89 x 116 cm
*National Museum of Western Art, Tokyo*

**90 • Breton Peasant with Pigs, 1888**
Oil on canvas, 73 x 93 cm
*Lucille Ellis Simon Collection, Los Angeles*

**91 • Winter or Breton Child Putting on His Clogs, 1888**
Oil on canvas, 90 x 71 cm
*Ny Carlsberg Glyptotek, Copenhagen*

**92 • The Aven, 1888**
Oil on canvas, 73 x 93 cm
*Bridgestone Museum, Tokyo*

**93 • Meadow on the Banks of the Aven, 1888**
Oil on canvas, 60 x 73 cm
*Private Collection*

**94 • The Turkeys, 1888**
Oil on canvas, 92 x 73 cm

**95 • Head of Breton Woman, 1888**
Oil on canvas, 33 x 24 cm
*Private Collection*

**96 • The Vision of the Sermon or Jacob Wrestling with the Angel, 1888**
Oil on canvas, 73 x 92 cm
*National Gallery of Scotland, Edinburgh*

WORKS

**97 • Ring of Breton Girls, 1888**
Oil on canvas, 71.4 x 92.8 cm
*National Gallery of Art, Washington*

**98 • Bretons and Bull, 1888**
Oil on canvas, 91 x 72 cm
*Ny Carlsberg Glyptotek, Copenhagen*

**99 • The Aven at Pont-Aven, 1888**
Oil on canvas, 72 x 93 cm
*Koerfer Collection, Bern*

**100 • Woman with a Pitcher or
Landscape at Pont-Aven, 1888**
Oil on canvas, 92 x 72 cm
*Private Collection*

**101 • Line Fishermen, 1888**
Oil on canvas, 72 x 60 cm
*Private Collection*

**102 • The White River, 1888**
Oil on canvas, 58 x 72 cm
*Musée de Grenoble, Grenoble*

**103 • Fishermen and Bathers
on the Aven, 1888**
Oil on canvas, 73 x 60 cm
*Private Collection*

**104 • Dog Racing, 1888**
Oil on canvas, 92 x 71 cm
*Private Collection*

**105 • The Port of Aven, 1888**
Oil on canvas, 73 x 92 cm
*Private Collection*

**106 • Willow on the Banks
of the Water, 1888**
Oil on canvas, 74 x 60 cm
*Private Collection*

**107 • Small Creek Before Pont-Aven
Port, 1888**
Oil on canvas, 92 x 73 cm
*Ordrupgaard Collection, Copenhagen*

**108 • Harvest in Brittany, 1888**
Oil on canvas, 73 x 92 cm
*Musée d'Orsay, Paris*

97    98
99    100    101
102    103
104    105
106    107    108

109

110

111

112

113

114

115

116

117

118

119

120

**109 • Flowers in Front of a Window Open to the Sea, 1888**
Oil on canvas, 73 x 92 cm
*Musée d'Orsay, Paris*

**110 • Young Bretons Bathing, 1888 (?)**
Oil on canvas, 60 x 73 cm
*Private Collection*

**111 • Children Wrestling, 1888**
Oil on canvas, 93 x 73 cm
*Josefowitz Collection, Lausanne*

**112 • Young Bretons Bathing, 1888**
Oil on canvas, 92 x 73 cm
*Kunsthalle, Hamburg*

**113 • Landscape with Ducks, 1888**
Oil on canvas, 73 x 92 cm
*Private Collection*

**114 • Girl Tending Geese, 1888**
Oil on canvas, 24 x 38 cm
*Henderson Collection, New Orleans*

**115 • A Cow Lying Down, 1888**
Oil on canvas, 47 x 34 cm
*Private Collection*

**116 • The Cow and Her Calf, 1888**
Oil on canvas, 25 x 40 cm
*Private Collection*

**117 • The Creek, 1888**
Oil on canvas, 49 x 58 cm
*Josefowitz Collection, Lausanne*

**118 • A Clog Maker, 1888**
Oil on canvas, 58 x 49 cm
*Josefowitz Collection, Lausanne*

**119 • Cliffs in Brittany, 1888**
Oil on canvas, 59 x 92 cm
*Dessau Collection, Copenhagen*

**120 • Seascape with Cow on the Edge of a Cliff, 1888**
Oil on canvas, 73 x 60 cm
*Musée des Arts Décoratifs, Paris*

## WORKS

**121 • The Customs Officer's House, 1888**
Oil on canvas, 54 x 65 cm
*National Gallery of Art, Washington*

**122 • Farm and Cow, 1888**
Oil on canvas, 47 x 63 cm

**123 • The Wave, 1888**
Oil on canvas 49 x 58 cm
*Private Collection*

**124 • Apples and Pitcher, 1888**
Oil on canvas, 32 x 55 cm
*Oskar Reinhart Collection, Winterthur*

**125 • Still Life with Fruit, 1888**
Oil on canvas, 43 x 58 cm
*Pushkin Museum, Moscow*

**126 • Fruit Basket with Figure of Bather, 1887-1888**
Stoneware, 29 x 29 cm
*Sackler Collection*

**127 • Still Life with Ceramic, 1888**
Oil on canvas, 47 x 55 cm

**128 • Still Life: Fête Gloanec, 1888**
Oil on wood, 38 x 53 cm
*Musée des Beaux-Arts, Orléans*

**129 • Still Life for His Friend Jacob, 1888**
Oil on cardboard, 27 x 35 cm
*Jäggli-Hahnloser Collection, Winterthur*

**130 • Kitten with Three Apples, 1888**
Oil on canvas, 72 x 24 cm
*Private Collection*

**131 • Still Life with Three Puppies, 1888**
Oil on wood, 92 x 63 cm
*The Museum of Modern Art, New York*

**132 • Captain Jacob, 1888**
Oil on canvas, 31 x 43 cm
*Private Collection*

121

122

123

124

125

126

127

128

129

130

131

132

133

134

135

136

137

138

139

140

141

142

143

144

**133 • La Fiancée
(La Gudu, Hotel Waitress), 1888**
Oil on canvas, 33 x 41 cm
*Josefowitz Collection, Lausanne*

**134 • Portrait of Madeleine
Bernard, 1888**
Oil on canvas, 72 x 58 cm
*Musée de Grenoble*

**135 • Self-Portrait,
Les Misérables, 1888**
Oil on canvas, 45 x 55 cm
*Van Gogh Museum, Amsterdam*

**136 • Self-Portrait, 1888**
Oil on jute canvas, 46 x 38 cm
*Pushkin Museum, Moscow*

**137 • Vincent Van Gogh Painting
Sunflowers, 1888**
Oil on canvas, 73 x 92 cm
*Van Gogh Museum, Amsterdam*

**138 • Blue Trees, 1888**
Oil on canvas, 92 x 73 cm
*Ordrupgaard Collection, Copenhagen*

**139 • Landscape at Arles
with Bushes, 1888**
Oil on canvas, 73 x 92 cm
*Private Collection*

**140 • Farms at Arles, 1888**
Oil on canvas, 72 x 92 cm
*Nationalmuseum, Stockholm*

**141 • Washerwomen and Goat, 1888**
Oil on canvas, 73 x 92 cm
*Museo de Bellas Artes y de Arte
Moderno, Bilbao*

**142 • View of Les Alyscamps, 1888**
Oil on canvas, 73 x 93 cm
*Private Collection*

**143 • View of Les Alyscamps, 1888**
Oil on canvas, 92 x 73 cm
*Musée d'Orsay, Paris*

**144 • Farm at Arles, 1888**
Oil on canvas, 91 x 72 cm
*Museum of Art, Indianapolis*

**145 • The Laundresses, 1888**
Oil on canvas, 73 x 92 cm
*William S. Paley Collection, New York*

**146 • Human Misery or Grape Harvest (Arles), 1888**
Oil on canvas, 73 x 92 cm
*Ordrupgaard Collection, Copenhagen*

**147 • In the Hay, 1888**
Oil on canvas, 73 x 92 cm
*Private Collection*

**148 • Old Women at Arles, 1888**
Oil on canvas, 73 x 92 cm
*The Art Institute, Chicago*

**149 • Madame Ginoux at the Café, 1888**
Oil on canvas, 73 x 92 cm
*Pushkin Museum, Moscow*

**150 • Madame Roulin (Arles), 1888**
Oil on canvas, 49 x 62 cm
*City Art Museum, St. Louis*

**151 • Decorative Landscape, 1888 (?)**
Oil on canvas
*Nationalmuseum, Stockholm*

**152 • Still Life with Fan, 1889**
Oil on canvas, 50 x 61 cm
*Musée d'Orsay, Paris*

**153 • The Schuffenecker Family, 1889**
Oil on canvas, 73 x 92 cm
*Musée d'Orsay, Paris*

**154 • Christ in the Garden of Olives (Self Portrait), 1889**
Oil on canvas, 73 x 92 cm
*Norton Gallery and School of Art, West Palm Beach*

**155 • The Green Christ, 1889**
Oil on canvas, 92 x 73 cm
*Musées Royaux d'Art et d'Histoire, Brussels*

**156 • The Yellow Christ, 1889**
Oil on canvas, 92 x 73 cm
*Albright-Knox Art Gallery, Buffalo*

145

146

147

148

149

150

151

152

153

154

155

156

157

158

159

160

161

162

163

164

165

166

167

168

**157 • Self-Portrait with Yellow Christ, 1889-1890**
Oil on canvas, 38 x 46 cm
*Private Collection*

**158 • Madame Kohler
(Marie Henry. Jeanne Gloanec),
1889**
Oil on cardboard, 46 x 38 cm
*National Gallery of Art, Washington*

**159 • La Belle Angèle, 1889**
Oil on canvas, 92 x 73 cm
*Musée d'Orsay, Paris*

**160 • Young Breton Girl, 1889**
Oil on canvas, 46 x 38 cm
*Ascoli Collection, New York*

**161 • In the Waves or Ondine, 1889**
Oil on canvas, 92 x 72 cm
*The Museum of Art, Cleveland*

**162 • Life and Death, 1889**
Oil on canvas, 92 x 73 cm
*Mahmoud Khalil Bey Museum, Cairo*

**163 • Nude Breton Boy, 1889**
Oil on canvas, 93 x 73.5 cm
*Wallraf-Richartz Museum, Cologne*

**164 • Girl Tending Cows, 1889**
Oil on canvas, 72 x 91 cm
*Ny Carlsberg Glyptotek, Copenhagen*

**165 • Harvest in Brittany, 1889**
Oil on canvas, 92 x 73 cm
*Courtauld Institute Galleries, London*

**166 • Peasants Tossing the Hay, 1889**
Oil on canvas, 76 x 95 cm
*Private Collection*

**167 • Yellow Haystacks,
or The Blond Grain, 1889**
Oil on canvas, 73.5 x 92.5 cm
*Musée d'Orsay, Paris*

**168 • The Willow, 1889**
Oil on canvas, 92 x 73 cm
*Private Collection*

## WORKS

**169 • The Willows, 1889**
Oil on canvas, 92 x 73 cm
*Nasjonalgalleriet, Oslo*

**170 • Young Breton
with Goose, 1889**
Oil on canvas, 92 x 73 cm
*Blaffer Collection, Houston*

**171 • The Barrier, 1889**
Oil on canvas, 92 x 73 cm
*Private Collection*

**172 • Sewing, 1889**
Oil on canvas, 73 x 92 cm
*Bührle Collection, Zurich*

**173 • The Fields on
the Seashore, 1889**
Oil on canvas, 72 x 91 cm
*Nationalmuseum, Stockholm*

**174 • Girl Tending Pigs, 1889**
Oil on canvas, 73 x 92 cm
*Private Collection*

**175 • Red Cow, 1889**
Oil on canvas, 92 x 73 cm
*County Museum of Art, Los Angeles*

**176 • Sentimental Stroll, 1889**
Oil on canvas, 90 x 72 cm
*Vanderbilt Webb Collection, New York*

**177 • Among the Lillies, 1889**
Oil on canvas, 92 x 73 cm
*Rudolf Staechelin Foundation, Basel*

**178 • The Undersea Cliff, 1889**
Oil on canvas
*Private Collection*

**179 • The Flute Player on
the Cliff, 1889**
Oil on canvas, 73 x 92 cm
*Private Collection*

**180 • The Isolated House 1889**
Oil on canvas, 60 x 73 cm
*Josten Collection, New York*

169

170

171

172

173

174

175

176

177

178

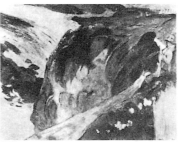
179

180

181

182

183

184

185

186

187

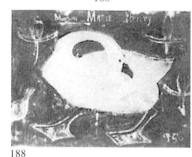
188

189

190

191

192

**181 • The Seaweed Gatherers, 1889**
Oil on canvas, 87 x 122.5 cm
*Folkwang Museum, Essen*

**182 • The Seaweed Gatherers, 1889**
Oil on cardboard mounted on canvas,
14 x 17 cm
*Fujikawa Gallery, Osaka*

**183 • Pouldu Beach, 1889**
Oil on canvas, 73 x 92 cm
*Private Collection*

**184 • On the Beach (Brittany), 1889**
Oil on canvas, 60 x 73 cm
*Nasjonalgalleriet, Oslo*

**185 • Breton Girls by the Sea, 1889**
Oil on canvas, 92 x 73 cm
*National Museum of Western Art,
Tokyo*

**186 • Girls at the Pouldu, 1889**
Oil on canvas, 93 x 74 cm
*Private Collection*

**187 • Young Girl Spining Wool, 1889**
Oil, 116 x 58 cm
*Private Collection*

**188 • The Goose, 1889**
Oil on canvas, 48 x 56 cm
*Levy Collection, New York*

**189 • Caribbean Woman, 1889**
Oil on wood, 64 x 54 cm
*Bakwin Collection, New York*

**190 • Lust, 1889**
Wood, 70 cm
*Willumsen Museet, Frederikssund*

**191 • Bonjour Monsieur
Gauguin, 1889**
Oil on canvas, 113 x 92 cm
*Národni Gallery, Prague*

**192 • Nirvana, Portrait of Jacob
Meyer de Haan, 1889**
Oil on silk, 20 x 29.2 cm
*Wadsworth Atheneum, Hartford*

## WORKS

**193 • Self-Portrait, 1889**
Oil on wood, 79.6 x 51.7 cm
*National Gallery of Art, Washington*

**194 • Meyer de Haan, 1889**
Oil on canvas, 80 x 52 cm
*Private Collection*

**195 • Still Life with Onions, 1889**
Oil on canvas mounted on cardboard,
39 x 50 cm
*Ny Carlsberg Glyptotek, Copenhagen*

**196 • Jug in the Form of a Head,
Self-Portrait, 1889**
Glazed stoneware, 19.3 cm
*Kunstindustrimuseet, Copenhagen*

**197 • Still Life with Japanese Print,
or Still Life with Vase in the Shape
of a Head, 1889**
Oil on canvas, 73 x 92 cm
*Museum of Modern Art, Teheran*

**198 • Still Life "Ripipoint", 1889**
Oil on canvas, 32.5 x 40 cm
*Blum-Lowy Collection, Shorthills
(New Jersey)*

**199 • Still Life with Peaches, 1889**
Oil on canvas, 25 x 32 cm
*The Fogg Art Museum, Cambridge
(Massachusetts)*

**200 • The Ham, 1889**
Oil on canvas, 50 x 58 cm
*The Phillips Collection, Washington*

**201 • Still Life,
"À la comtesse de N. ", 1889**
Oil on canvas, 49 x 55 cm
*Kennedy Collection, London*

**202 • Soyez amoureuses, vous
serez heureuses (Be in Love and
You Will Be Happy), 1889**
Carved and painted lindenwood,
119 x 97 cm
*Museum of Fine Arts, Boston*

**203 • Bust of Meyer de Haan, 1889**
Polychromed oak wood, 57 cm
*National Gallery of Canada, Ottawa*

**204 • The Man with the Stick, 1889 (?)**
Oil on canvas, 70 x 45 cm
*Musée du Petit Palais, Paris*

193

194

195

196

197

198

199

200

201

202

203

204

205

206

207

208

209

210

211

212

213

214

215

216

**205 • Still Life with Flowers and Fruit, 1890 (?)**
Oil on canvas, 43 x 63 cm
*Museum of Fine Arts, Boston*

**206 • Fruit Bowl on a Garden Chair, 1890**
Oil on canvas, 28 x 37 cm
*County Museum, Los Angeles*

**207 • Still Life with Blue Fruit Bowl, 1890**
Oil on canvas, 23 x 30 cm
*National Gallery of Art, Washington*

**208 • Oranges and Lemons with View of Pont-Aven, 1890**
Oil on canvas, 50 x 61 cm
*Brown-Bovery Collection, Baden*

**209 • Still Life with Fruit and Vase Before a Window, 1890**
Oil on canvas, 50 x 61 cm
*Private Collection*

**210 • Apples, Pear, and Ceramic, 1890**
Oil on canvas, 28 x 36 cm
*The Fogg Art Museum, Cambridge (Massachusetts)*

**211 • Roses and Statuette, 1890**
Oil on canvas, 73 x 54 cm
*Musée des Beaux-Arts, Reims*

**212 • The Painter Slewinsky, 1890 or 1894 (?)**
Oil on canvas, 54 x 81 cm
*Bridgestone Art Museum, Tokyo*

**213 • Monsieur Loulou (Louis Le Ray), 1890**
Oil on canvas, 55 x 46.2 cm
*The Barnes Foundation, Merion*

**214 • Portrait of the Artist's Mother, 1890**
Oil on canvas, 41 x 33 cm
*Staatsgalerie, Stuttgart*

**215 • Eve Exotic, 1890**
Oil on cardboard, 43 x 25 cm
*Private Collection*

**216 • Adam and Eve or Paradise Lost, 1890**
Oil on canvas, 46 x 55 cm
*Yale University Art Gallery, New Haven*

## WORKS

**217 • The Haystacks or
The Potato Field, 1890**
Oil on canvas, 73 x 92 cm
*National Gallery of Art, Washington*

**218 • Bathers on the Beach, 1890**
Oil on canvas, 73 x 92 cm
*Private Collection*

**219 • Cornfields by the Seashore, 1890**
Oil on canvas, 73 x 92 cm
*The Tate Gallery, London*

**220 • La Maison du Pan du, 1890**
Oil on canvas, 51 x 61 cm
*Hammer Collection*

**221 • Landscape at Le Pouldu, 1890**
Oil on canvas, 54 x 65 cm
*Private Collection*

**222 • Fields at Pouldu, 1890**
Oil on canvas, 73 x 92 cm
*National Gallery of Art, Washington*

**223 • Farm at Le Pouldu, 1890**
Oil on canvas, 71 x 88 cm
*Museum of Art, Dallas*

**224 • Entrance to the Farm, 1890**
Oil on canvas, 92 x 73 cm
*Staatliche Kunsthalle, Karlsruhe*

**225 • Soyez mystérieuses
(Be Mysterious), 1890**
Carved and painted lindenwood,
73 x 95 x 0.5 cm
*Musée d'Orsay, Paris*

**226 • Portrait of a Woman,
with Still Life by Cézanne, 1890 (?)**
Oil on canvas, 65.3 x 54.9 cm
*The Art Institute, Chicago*

**227 • The Loss of Virginity, 1890-1891**
Oil on canvas, 90 x 130 cm
*The Chrysler Museum, Norfolk,
Virginia*

**228 • Copy of Manet's
Olympia, 1891**
Oil on canvas, 89 x 130 cm
*Private Collection*

217

218

219

220

221

222

223

224

225

226

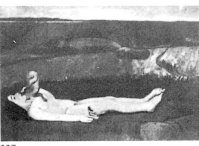
227

228

229     230     231

232     233     234

235     236

237     238

239     240

**229 • Self-Portrait with Idol, 1891**
Oil on canvas, 46 x 33 cm
*The Marion Koogler Mc Nay Art Institute, San Antonio (Texas)*

**230 • Idol, 1891 (?)**
Wood, 40 cm
*Brooks Collection*

**231 • Young Man with Flower, 1891**
Oil on canvas, 46 x 33 cm
*Private Collection*

**232 • Head of a Tahitian Woman (La Fleur qui écoute), 1891**
Oil on canvas, 30 x 25 cm
*Spaulding Collection, Boston*

**233 • Vahine no te Tiare (Girl with a Flower), 1891**
Oil on canvas, 70 x 46 cm
*Ny Carlsberg Glyptotek, Copenhagen*

**234 • Portrait of Suzanne Bambridge, 1891**
Oil on canvas, 70 x 50 cm
*Musées Royaux d'Art et d'Histoire, Brussels*

**235 • Captain Swaton, 1891**
Oil on canvas, 45 x 36 cm
*Private Collection*

**236 • Head of a Young Mulatto, 1891**
Oil on canvas, 36 x 30 cm
*Musée des Beaux-Arts, Troyes*

**237 • Te tiare farani (Flowers of France), 1891**
Oil on canvas, 72 x 92 cm
*Pushkin Museum, Moscow*

**238 • The Meal or The Bananas, 1891**
Oil on canvas, 73 x 92 cm
*Musée d'Orsay, Paris*

**239 • Still Life on Tablecloth, 1891**
Oil on canvas, 36 x 48 cm
*The Metropolitan Museum of Art, New York*

**240 • Parau Parau (Gossiping), 1891**
Oil on canvas, 62 x 92 cm
*The Hermitage Museum, St. Petersburg*

# WORKS

**241 • Upaupa (Feast), 1891**
Oil on canvas, 73 x 92 cm
*Israel Museum, Jerusalem*

**242 • Te raau rahi
(The Big Tree), 1891**
Oil on canvas, 72 x 92 cm
*The Art Institute, Chicago*

**243 • Te raau rahi, 1891**
Oil on canvas, 73 x 92 cm
*The Museum of Art, Cleveland*

**244 • Te Fare maorie
(The Maori's House), 1891**
Oil on canvas, 73 x 92 cm
*Roniger Collection, Rheinfelden*

**245 • The Meeting, 1891**
Oil on canvas, 73 x 91 cm
*The Solomon R. Guggenheim Museum,
New York*

**246 • Haere mai (Come), 1891**
Oil on canvas, 74 x 92 cm
*The Solomon R. Guggenheim Museum,
New York*

**247 • The Little Black Pigs, 1891**
Oil on canvas, 91 x 72 cm
*Museum of Fine Arts, Budapest*

**248 • Road to Papeete (?)
or Street in Tahiti, 1891**
Oil on canvas, 115.5 x 88.5 cm
*Museum of Art, Toledo (Ohio)*

**249 • Horse Grazing, 1891**
Oil on canvas, 64 x 47 cm
*The Metropolitan Museum of Art,
New York*

**250 • Bathers, 1891**
Oil on canvas, 92 x 73 cm
*Private Collection*

**251 • The Man with an Axe, 1891**
Oil on canvas, 92 x 69 cm
*Private Collection*

**252 • I raro te
(Under the Pandanus), 1891**
Oil on canvas, 68 x 90 cm
*Museum of Arts, Dallas*

241   242   243   244   245   246   247   248   249   250   251   252

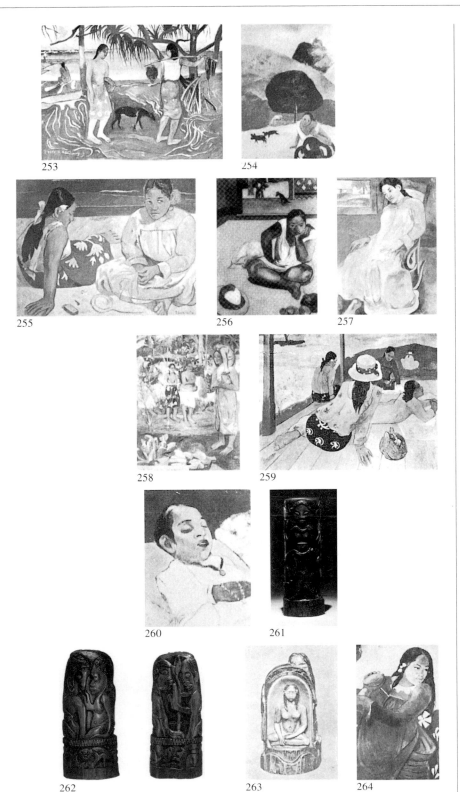

253

254

255

256

257

258

259

260

261

262

263

264

**253 • I raro te
(Under the Pandanus), 1891**
Oil on canvas, 73 x 92 cm
*The Institute of Arts, Minneapolis*

**254 • Landscape with
Tahitian Woman, 1891**
Oil on canvas, 37 x 27 cm

**255 • Tahitian Women or
On the Beach, 1891**
Oil on canvas, 69 x 91 cm
*Musée d'Orsay, Paris*

**256 • Te faaturuma (Silence), 1891**
Oil on canvas, 91 x 68 cm
*Art Museum, Worcester*

**257 • Faaturuma (Dreams or
Woman in a Red Dress), 1891**
Oil on canvas, 94.6 x 68.6 cm
*Nelson Atkins Museum of Art, Kansas
City*

**258 • Ia orana Maria (Hail Mary),
1891-1892**
Oil on canvas, 113.7 x 87.7 cm
*The Metropolitan Museum of Art,
New York*

**259 • The Siesta, c. 1891-1892**
Oil on canvas, 87 x 116 cm
*Mr. and Mrs. Walter H. Annenberg
Collection, Palm Springs*

**260 • Atiti; Dead child
(Aristide Suhas), 1892**
Oil on canvas, 30 x 25 cm
*Rijksmuseum Kröller-Müller, Otterlo*

**261 • Cylinder Decorated with
Representation of Hina, 1892 (?)**
Polychromed and gilded Tamanu
wood, 37.1 x 10.8 cm
*Hirshhorn Museum and Sculpture
Garden, Washington*

**262 • Hina and Fatou, 1892 (?)**
Tamanu wood, 32.7 x 14.2 cm
*Art Gallery of Ontario, Toronto*

**263 • Idol with a Pearl, 1892 (?)**
Polychromed and gilded, pearl and
gold Tamanu wood, 25 x 12 cm
*Musée d'Orsay, Paris*

**264 • Vahine no te vi
(Woman with Mango), 1892**
Oil on canvas, 72.7 x 44.5 cm
*The Museum of Art, Baltimore*

## WORKS

**265 • Nafea faaipoipo
(When will you get married?), 1892**
Oil on canvas, 105 x 77.5 cm
*Rudolf Staechelin Foundation, Basel*

**266 • Parau hanohano
(Terrifying Words), 1892**
Oil on canvas
*Private Collection*

**267 • Primitive Tales, 1892**
Oil on canvas, 39 x 28 cm
*Private Collection*

**268 • Parau na te Varua ino
(Words from the Devil), 1892**
Oil on canvas, 91.7 x 68.5 cm
*National Gallery of Art, Washington*

**269 • Two Tahitian Women
on the Beach, 1892**
Oil on canvas, 91 x 64 cm
*Academy of Arts, Honolulu*

**270 • Vahine no te miti
(Women Sea), 1892**
Oil on canvas, 93 x 74.5 cm
*Museo Nacional de Bellas Artes,
Buenos Aires*

**271 • Manao Tupapau
(The Spirit of the Dead is
Watching), 1892**
Oil on canvas, 73 x 92 cm
*Albright-Knox Art Gallery, Buffalo*

**272 • Te aa no areois
(The Seed of the Ariois), 1892**
Oil on canvas, 92 x 78 cm
*William S. Paley Collection, New York*

**273 • Idol with a Shell, 1892**
Toa wood, nacre and bone, 27 x 14 cm
*Musée d'Orsay, Paris*

**274 • Vairumati tei oa
(The Name is Vairumati), 1892**
Oil on canvas, 91 x 60 cm
*Pushkin Museum, Moscow*

**275 • Te nave nave fenua
(The Delightful Land), 1892**
Oil on canvas, 91 x 72 cm
*Ohara Museum of Art, Kurashiki*

**276 • Arii Matamoe (Royal End), 1892**
Oil on canvas, 45 x 75 cm
*Private Collection*

265

266

267

268

269

270

271

272

273

274

275

276

277

278

279

280

281

282

283

284

285

286

287

288

**277 • Carving of Tehamana, 1892 (?)**
Polychromed and gilded Pua wood,
25 x 20 cm
*Musée d'Orsay, Paris*

**278 • Aha oe feii ?
(What! Are You Jealous?), 1892**
Oil on canvas, 68 x 92 cm
*Pushkin Museum, Moscow*

**279 • Tahitian Women Bathing, 1892**
Oil on canvas, 112 x 89 cm
*The Metropolitan Museum of Art,
New York*

**280 • Haere Pape
(Morning Cleaning), 1892**
Oil on canvas, 90 x 67 cm
*The Barnes Foundation, Merion*

**281 • Women at the Riverside, 1892**
Oil on canvas, 32 x 40 cm
*Private Collection*

**282 • Fatata te miti
(Near the Sea), 1892**
Oil on canvas, 68 x 92 cm
*National Gallery of Art, Washington*

**283 • Parau Api
(The News of the Day), 1892**
Oil on canvas, 67 x 91 cm
*Gemäldegalerie Neue Meister,
Dresden*

**284 • Te fare hymenee
(The House of Songs), 1892**
Oil on canvas, 50 x 90 cm
*Meadows Collection, Dallas*

**285 • Valley with Trees, 1892**
Oil on canvas, 42 x 67 cm
*Jäggli-Hahnloser Collection,
Winterthur*

**286 • Mau Taporo
(The Lemon Harvest), 1892**
Oil on canvas, 89 x 66 cm
*Goulandris Collection, New York*

**287 • Tahitian Town, 1892**
Oil on canvas, 90 x 70 cm
*Ny Carlsberg Glyptotek, Copenhagen*

**288 • Parau Parau
(Conversation), 1892**
Oil on canvas, 76 x 56 cm
*Whitney Collection, New York*

# WORKS

**289 • Te fare (The House), 1892**
Oil on canvas, 73 x 92 cm
*Private Collection*

**290 • Fatata te mouà
(The Mountain is Near), 1892**
Oil on canvas, 68 x 92 cm
*The Hermitage Museum,
St. Petersburg*

**291 • Women at the Riverside, 1892**
Oil on canvas, 43 x 31 cm
*Van Gogh Museum, Amsterdam*

**292 • Noa Noa. Scented Nature, 1892**
Oil on canvas, 92 x 73 cm
*Private Collection*

**293 • Te Bourao (The Big Tree), 1892**
Oil on canvas, 67 x 89 cm
*The Art Institute, Chicago*

**294 • Dog in front of the Cabin
or The Three Cabins, 1892**
Oil on canvas, 35 x 55 cm
*Penteado Collection, São Paulo*

**295 • Matamoe. Landscape
with Peacocks, 1892**
Oil on canvas, 115 x 86 cm
*Pushkin Museum, Moscow*

**296 • Te Poipoi (The Morning), 1892**
Oil on canvas, 68 x 92 cm
*Payson Collection, New York*

**297 • Soumin (Blue Ibis), 1892**
Essence and turpentine mounted on
canvas, 89 x 58 cm

**298 • Matamua (Bygone Times), 1892**
Oil on canvas, 93 x 72 cm
*Private Collection*

**299 • Arearea (Amusement), 1892**
Oil on canvas, 75 x 94 cm
*Musée d'Orsay, Paris*

**300 • Tahitian Pastorals, 1892**
Oil on canvas, 87.5 x 113.7 cm
*The Hermitage Museum,
St. Petersburg*

289

290

291

292

293

294

295

296

297

298

299

300

301

302

303

304

305

306

307

308

309

310

311

312

**301 • Ta Matete
(The Marketplace), 1892**
Gouache on canvas, 73 x 92 cm
*Kunstmuseum, Basel*

**302 • E Haere oe i hia
(Where are you Going), 1892**
Oil on canvas, 96 x 69 cm
*Staatsgalerie, Stuttgart*

**303 • Cabin Under the Trees, 1892**
Oil on canvas, 72 x 43 cm
*Otten Collection, West Englewood*

**304 • Parahi te marae
(There Stands the Srine), 1892**
Oil on canvas, 68 x 91 cm
*Philadelphia Museum of Art,
Philadephia*

**305 • Apples and hot peppers, 1892**
Oil on canvas, 31 x 65 cm

**306 • Head of a Tahitian Women,
1892 (?)**
Oil on canvas, 41 x 27 cm
*Geiser Collection, Basel*

**307 • Landscape with Three Trees,
1892 (?)**
Oil on canvas, 60 x 92 cm
*Robert Lehman Foundation, New York*

**308 • Tahitian Woman with Naked
Torso and Fruit, 1892 (?)**
Oil on glass, 100 x 54 cm
*Berman Collection*

**309 • Ea Haere ia oe
(Where are you Going?), 1893 (?)**
Oil on canvas, 91 x 72 cm
*The Hermitage Museum, St.
Petersburg*

**310 • Merahi metua no Tehamana
(Tehamana has many Parents), 1893**
Oil on canvas, 76 x 54 cm
*The Art Institute, Chicago*

**311 • Mountains in Tahiti, 1893**
Oil on canvas, 67.8 x 92.4 cm
*The Institute of Arts, Minneapolis*

**312 • Apatarao, 1893**
Oil on canvas, 49 x 54 cm
*Ny Carlsberg Glyptotek, Copenhagen*

**313 • Tahitian Near a Stream, 1893**
Oil on canvas, 73 x 92 cm
*Halphen Collection, Paris*

**314 • Hina Maruru
(Celebration for Hina), 1893**
Oil on canvas, 93 x 70 cm
*Private Collection*

**315 • Otahi (Alone), 1893**
Oil on canvas, 50 x 73 cm
*Private Collection*

**316 • Pape Moe
(Mysterious Water), 1893**
Oil on canvas, 99 x 75 cm
*Private Collection*

**317 • Hina Tefatou
(The Moon and Earth), 1893**
Oil on canvas, 112 x 61 cm
*The Musem of Modern Art, New York*

**318 • Tahitian in Landscape, 1893**
Oil on glass, 116 x 75 cm
*Musée d'Orsay, Paris*

**319 • Nave nave. Vegetable
and Floral Motives, 1893**
Oil on glass, 105 x 75 cm
*Musée d'Orsay, Paris*

**320 • Rupe Tahiti, 1893**
Oil on glass, 181 x 71 cm
*Private Collection*

**321 • Aita tamari vahine Judith
te parari (The Child-Woman Judith
is not yet Breached) or Annah
the Javanese, 1893-1894**
Oil on canvas, 116 x 81 cm
*Private Collection*

**322 • Portrait of William Molard,
1893-1894**
Oil on canvas, 46 x 38 cm
*Musée d'Orsay, Paris*

**323 • Self-Portrait with Hat,
1893-1894**
Oil on canvas, 46 x 38 cm
*Musée d'Orsay, Paris*

**324 • Self-Portrait with Palette,
c. 1894**
Oil on canvas, 92 x 73 cm
*Private Collection*

313

314

315

316

317

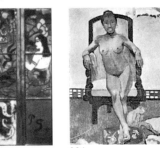
318

319

320

321

322

323

324

325

326

327

328

329

330

331

332

333

334

335

336

**325 • Young Tahitian with Pink Sarong, 1894**
Brush and gouache on cardboard, 25 x 24 cm
*William S. Paley Collection, New York*

**326 • Mahana no atua (Day of the God), 1894**
Oil on canvas, 68.3 x 91.5 cm
*The Art Institute, Chicago*

**327 • Nave Nave moe (Enjoying a Rest), 1894**
Oil on canvas, 73 x 98 cm
*The Hermitage Museum, St. Petersburg*

**328 • Tahitiennes au repos, 1894**
Charcoal on paper, 85.5 x 102 cm
*The Tate Gallery, London*

**329 • Arearea no varua ino (Under the Spirit Power), 1894**
Oil on canvas, 60 x 98 cm
*Ny Carlsberg Glyptotek, Copenhagen*

**330 • Upaupa Schneklud, 1894**
Oil on canvas, 92.5 x 73.5 cm
*The Museum of Art, Baltimore*

**331 • The Young Christian Girl or Little Girl in Yellow, 1894**
Oil on canvas, 65 x 46 cm
*Sterling and Francine Clark Art Institute, Williamstown (Massachusetts)*

**332 • Drama in the Town, 1894**
Oil on canvas, 92 x 70 cm
*Private Collection*

**333 • Farm in Brittany, 1894**
Oil on canvas,
*Private Collection*

**334 • Farm in Brittany, 1894**
Oil on canvas, 73 x 92 cm
*The Metropolitan Museum of Art, New York*

**335 • The Moulin David in Pont-Aven, 1894**
Oil on canvas, 73 x 92 cm
*Musée d'Orsay, Paris*

**336 • Christmas Night, 1894**
Oil on canvas, 72 x 83 cm
*Private Collection*

## WORKS

**337 • Village in the Snow, 1894**
Oil on canvas, 76 x 66 cm
*Private Collection*

**338 • Breton Village Under the Snow, 1894**
Oil on canvas, 62 x 87 cm
*Musée d'Orsay, Paris*

**339 • Peasant with His Dog Near a Gate, 1894**
Oil on canvas, 92 x 70 cm
*Private Collection*

**340 • Two Breton Peasants, 1894**
Oil on canvas, 66 x 92 cm
*Musée d'Orsay, Paris*

**341 • Paris Under the Snow, 1894**
Oil on canvas, 71.5 x 88 cm
*Van Gogh Museum, Amsterdam*

**342 • The Laundresses, 1894**
Oil on canvas, 99 x 72 cm
*Mac Kay Collection*

**343 • (Wild), 1894**
Glazed ceramic, 57 x 19 x 27 cm
*Musée d'Orsay, Paris*

**344 • Te raau rahi. Painted Fan, 1894 (?)**
Gouache on paper
*Carrick Hill Collection, Australia*

**345 • Fan Decorated with Motifs from Arearea (Amusement), 1894 or 1895**
Gouache on fabric, 26 x 55.3 cm
*The Museum of Fine Arts, Houston*

**346 • Self-Portrait, (Savage), 1894-1895**
Bronze, 36 x 36 cm
*Private Collection*

**347 • Child with Bib, 1895**
Oil on canvas, 32 x 25 cm
*Private Collection*

**348 • Portrait of Two Children, 1895 (1890 ? )**
Oil on canvas, 46 x 61 cm
*Ny Carlsberg Glyptotek, Copenhagen*

337

338

339

340

341

342

343

344

345

346

347

348

349

350

351

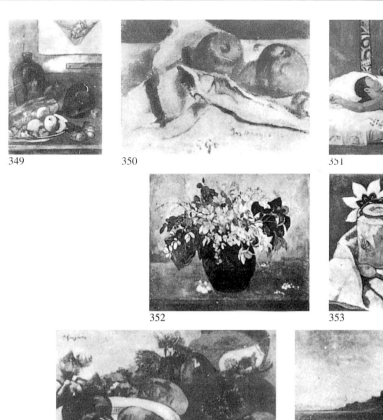

352

353

354

355

356

357

358

359

360

**349 • Still Life with Delacroix Engraving, 1895**
Oil on canvas, 40 x 30 cm
*Musée des Beaux-Arts, Strasbourg*

**350 • Still Life, "pas manger li", 1895 (?)**
Oil on canvas, 19 x 26 cm
*Musée des Beaux-Arts, Reims*

**351 • Te tamari no atua (The Birth of Christ), 1896**
Oil on canvas, 96 x 128 cm
*Neue Pinakothek, Munich*

**352 • Vase with Red Flowers, 1896**
Oil on canvas, 63 x 73 cm
*The Tate Gallery, London*

**353 • Tea Urn and Fruits, 1896**
Oil on canvas, 48 x 66 cm
*Mr. and Mrs. Walter H. Annenberg Collection, New York*

**354 • Still Life with Mangoes, 1896**
Oil on canvas

**355 • Landscape of Te Vaa, 1896**
Oil on canvas, 46 x 74 cm
*Musée des Beaux-Arts, Le Havre*

**356 • The Boat, 1896**
Oil on canvas, 50 x 36 cm
*Braye Collection, Paris*

**357 • Poor Fishermen, 1896**
Oil on canvas, 76 x 66 cm
*Museu de Arte, São Paulo*

**358 • Te Vaa (The Canoe), 1896**
Oil on canvas, 96 x 130 cm
*The Hermitage Museum, St. Petersburg*

**359 • Te arii Vahine (The Noble Woman or Woman with Mangoes), 1896**
Oil on canvas, 97 x 130 cm
*Pushkin Museum, Moscow*

**360 • Te arii Vahine, 1896**
Oil on canvas, 27 x 32 cm

## WORKS

**361 • Three Tahitian Women, 1896**
Oil on wood, 24.7 x 43.2 cm
*Haupt Collection, New York*

**362 • A Scene of Tahitian Life, 1896**
Oil on canvas, 89 x 124 cm
*The Hermitage Museum, St. Petersburg*

**363 • Nave nave mahana (Delightful Day), 1896**
Oil on canvas, 95 x 130 cm
*Musée des Beaux-Arts, Lyon*

**364 • No te aha oe riri (Why are you Angry ?), 1896**
Oil on canvas, 95 x 130 cm
*The Art Institute, Chicago*

**365 • Tahitian Nativity (Bé Bé), 1896**
Oil on canvas, 66 x 75 cm
*The Hermitage Museum, St. Petersburg*

**366 • Primitive Poems, 1896**
Oil on canvas, 65 x 48 cm
*The Fogg Art Museum, Cambridge (Massachusetts)*

**367 • Eiaha ohipa (Don't Work), 1896**
Oil on canvas, 65 x 75 cm
*The Hermitage Museum, St. Petersburg*

**368 • Joseph and Potiphar's Wife, 1896**
Oil on canvas, 88.3 x 117.5 cm
*Private Collection*

**369 • Portrait of Vaïté (Jeanne) Goupil, 1896**
Oil on canvas, 75 x 65 cm
*Ordrupgaard Collection, Copenhagen*

**370 • Self-Portrait Near Golgotha, 1896**
Oil on canvas, 76 x 64 cm
*Museu de Arte, São Paulo*

**371 • Self-Portrait for Daniel, 1896**
Oil on canvas, 40.5 x 32 cm
*Musée d'Orsay, Paris*

**372 • Nevermore, 1897**
Oil on canvas, 60.5 x 116 cm
*Courtauld Institute Galleries, London*

361

362

363

364

365

366

367

368

369

370

371

372

373

374

375

376

377

378

379

380

381

382

383

384

**373 • Bathers, 1897**
Oil on canvas, 60.4 x 93.4 cm
*National Gallery of Art, Washington*

**374 • Where Do We Come From?
What Are We? Where Are
We Going To?, 1897-1898**
Oil on canvas, 139 x 374.5 cm
*Museum of Fine Arts, Boston*

**375 • Tahiti. Sketches of Personages
for (Who are We?), 1897**
Oil on canvas, 92 x 73 cm
*Private Collection*

**376 • Te rerioa (The Dream), 1897**
Oil on canvas, 95 x 130
cm
*Courtauld Institute Galleries, London*

**377 • Rupe Rupe (The Harvest), 1897**
Oil on canvas, 92 x 73 cm
*The Hermitage Museum,
St. Petersburg*

**378 • Farari maruru (?)
Landscape with Two Goats, 1897**
Oil on canvas, 92 x 73 cm
*The Hermitage Museum, St.
Petersburg*

**379 • Te Bourao
(The Great Tree), 1897**
Oil on canvas, 73 x 92 cm
*Private Collection*

**380 • Vairumati, 1897**
Oil on canvas, 73 x 94 cm
*Musée d'Orsay, Paris*

**381 • Bathers in Tahiti, 1897**
Oil on canvas, 73 x 92 cm
*Barber Institute of Fine Arts,
Birmingham*

**382 • Faa ara (The Awakening), 1898**
Oil on canvas, 93 x 73 cm
*Ny Carlsberg Glyptotek, Copenhagen*

**383 • Te pape nave nave
(The Delicious), 1898**
Oil on canvas, 74 x 95.3 cm
*National Gallery of Art, Washington*

**384 • Faa Iheihe
(Tahitian Pastoral), 1898**
Oil on canvas, 54 x 169 cm
*The Tate Gallery, London*

## WORKS

**385 • The Idol, 1898**
Oil on canvas, 73 x 92 cm
*The Hermitage Museum,*
*St. Petersburg*

**386 • The White Horse, 1898**
Oil on canvas, 140 x 91 cm
*Musée d'Orsay, Paris*

**387 • Three Tahitians**
**or Conversation, 1898**
Oil on canvas, 73 x 93 cm
*National Gallery of Scotland,*
*Edinburgh*

**388 • Tahitian Woman, 1898**
Oil on canvas, 72 x 93 cm
*Ordrupgaard Collection, Copenhagen*

**389 • Tahitian Woman, 1898 (?)**
Oil on canvas, 93 x 130 cm
*Národni Muzej, Belgrade*

**390 • The Last Supper, 1897-1899**
Oil on canvas, 60 x 43.5 cm
*Granoff Collection, Paris*

**391 • Two Tahitian Women, 1899**
Oil on canvas, 94 x 72.2 cm
*The Metropolitan Museum of Art,*
*New York*

**392 • Portrait of a Woman**
**and a Young Man, 1899**
Oil on canvas, 95 x 61 cm
*Norton Simon Museum, Pasadena*

**393 • The Great Buddha, 1899**
Oil on canvas, 134 x 95 cm
*Pushkin Museum, Moscow*

**394 • Maternity, 1899**
Oil on cardboard mounted on canvas,
93 x 60 cm
*Rockefeller Collection, New York*

**395 • Motherhood or Women**
**on the Seashore, 1899**
Oil on canvas, 95.5 x 73.5 cm
*The Hermitage Museum,*
*St. Petersburg*

**396 • Te Avae no Maria**
**(The Month of Mary), 1899**
Oil on canvas, 94 x 72 cm
*The Hermitage Museum,*
*St. Petersburg*

385

386

387

388

389

390

391

392

393

394

395

396

397

398

399

400

401

402

403

404

405

406

407

408

**397 • Three Tahitians on a Background, 1899**
Oil on canvas, 69 x 74 cm
*The Hermitage Museum, St. Petersburg*

**398 • Rupe Rupe (Fruit Harvest), 1899**
Oil on canvas, 128 x 200 cm
*The Hermitage Museum, St. Petersburg*

**399 • Te tiai na oe ite rata (Are you Waiting for a Letter?), 1899**
Oil on canvas, 73 x 94 cm
*Private Collection*

**400 • Landscape with Horse, 1899**
Oil on canvas, 71 x 44 cm
*Shoenberg Collection, St. Louis*

**401 • Horse on a Path, 1899**
Oil on canvas, 94 x 73 cm
*Pushkin Museum, Moscow*

**402 • Cabin Under the Palm Trees, 1899**
Oil on canvas, 30 x 46 cm
*William S. Paley Collection, New York*

**403 • The Square Basket, 1899**
Oil on canvas, 61 x 73 cm
*Nasjonalgalleriet, Oslo*

**404 • Still Life with Cats, 1899**
Oil on canvas, 92 x 71 cm
*Ny Carlsberg Glyptotek, Copenhagen*

**405 • Bouquet of Flowers, 1899 (?)**
Oil on canvas, 95 x 62 cm
*Niarchos Collection, Athens*

**406 • Portraits of Women, 1899-1900**
Oil on canvas, 73 x 92 cm
*Private Collection*

**407 • Tea Urn, Vase, and Fruit, 1899**
Oil on canvas, 44 x 60 cm
*Israel Museum, Jerusalem*

**408 • Still Life with Knife, 1901**
Oil on canvas, 66 x 75 cm
*Bührle Collection, Zurich*

## WORKS

**409 • Flowers in a Vase, 1901**
Oil on canvas, 29 x 46 cm
*Cummings Collection, Chicago*

**410 • Mona Mona (Delicious), 1901**
Oil on canvas, 35 x 45 cm
*Peto Collection, London*

**411 • Still Life with Sunflowers
and Mangoes, 1901**
Oil on canvas, 93 x 73 cm
*Private Collection*

**412 • Still Life with Hope, 1901**
Oil on canvas, 65 x 77 cm
*Private Collection*

**413 • Sunflowers on
an Armchair, 1901**
Oil on canvas, 66 x 75 cm
*Bührle Collection, Zurich*

**414 • Sunflowers on an
Armchair, 1901**
Oil on canvas, 73 x 91 cm
*The Hermitage Museum,
St. Petersburg*

**415 • Woman and Children, 1901**
Oil on canvas, 97 x 74 cm
*The Art Institute, Chicago*

**416 • Golden Bodies, 1901**
Oil on canvas, 67 x 76 cm
*Musée d'Orsay, Paris*

**417 • Idyll on Tahiti, 1901**
Oil on canvas, 73 x 94 cm
*Bührle Collection, Zurich*

**418 • Landscape with Horses, 1901**
Oil on canvas, 95 x 63 cm
*Private Collection*

**419 • Near the Cabins, 1901**
Oil on canvas, 65 x 76 cm
*Carnegie Museum of Art, Pittsburgh*

**420 • The Horsemen
or The Ford, 1901**
Oil on canvas, 73 x 92 cm
*Pushkin Museum, Moscow*

409

410

411

412

413

414

415

416

417

418

419

420

421

422

423

424

425

426

427

428

429

430

431

432

**421 • Still Life with Apples and Flowers, 1901**
Oil on canvas, 66 x 76 cm
*Private Collection*

**422 • Flowers in a Vase, 1902**
Oil on canvas, 39 x 30 cm

**423 • Still Life with Exotic Birds, 1902**
Oil on canvas, 76 x 73 cm
*Von der Heydt Collection, Ascona*

**424 • Still Life with Exotic Birds, 1902**
Oil on canvas, 62 x 76 cm
*Pushkin Museum, Moscow*

**425 • Woman with a Fan, 1902**
Oil on canvas, 92 x 73 cm
*Folkwang Museum, Essen*

**426 • Guitar Player, 1902**
Oil on canvas, 90 x 72 cm
*Private Collection*

**427 • The Lovers (Idyll on Tahiti; The Escape), 1902**
Oil on canvas, 73 x 92.5 cm
*Národni Gallery, Prague*

**428 • Primitive Tales, 1902**
Oil on canvas, 131.5 x 90.5 cm
*Folkwang Museum, Essen*

**429 • Woman Seated in a Forest or Woman Crouching, 1902**
Oil on canvas
*Private Collection*

**430 • The Call, 1902**
Oil on canvas, 130 x 90 cm
*The Museum of Art, Cleveland*

**431 • Adam and Eve, 1902**
Oil on canvas, 59 x 38 cm
*Ordrupgaard Collection, Copenhagen*

**432 • Hiva Oa Man with Red Cape, 1902**
Oil on canvas, 92 x 73 cm
*Musée d'Art moderne, Liège*

## WORKS

**433 • The Enchantment, 1902**
Oil on canvas, 66 x 76 cm
*The Art Institute, Chicago*

**434 • Group of Figures
and Angel, 1902**
Oil on canvas, 26.5 x 45.5 cm
*Národni Gallery, Prague*

**435 • Bathers, 1902**
Oil on canvas, 92 x 73 cm
*Basil Goulandris Collection,
Lausanne*

**436 • The Sister of Charity, 1902**
Oil on canvas, 65 x 76 cm
*The Marion Koogler McNay Art
Institute, San Antonio*

**437 • Nativy, 1902**
Oil on canvas, 44 x 62 cm
*Wildenstein Collection, New York*

**438 • The Offering, 1902**
Oil on canvas, 68.5 x 78.5 cm
*Bührle Collection, Zurich*

**439 • Two Women or
The Flowered Headdress, 1902**
Oil on canvas, 72 x 60 cm
*Private Collection*

**440 • Horseman in Front
of a Shack, 1902**
Oil on canvas
*De Galea Collection*

**441 • Change of Residence, 1902**
Oil on canvas, 28 x 46 cm
*Nationalmuseum, Stockholm*

**442 • Riders on the Beach, 1902**
Oil on canvas, 66 x 76 cm
*Folkwang Museum, Essen*

**443 • Horsemen on the Beach, 1902**
Oil on canvas, 73 x 92 cm
*Private Collection*

**444 • The House of Pleasure:
Be Mysterious, 1902**
Carved and painted redwood,
40 x 153 cm
*Gauguin Museum, Papeari*

433

434

435

436

437

438

439

440

441

442

443

444

445

446

449

447       448       450

451                   452              453

**445 • The House of Pleasure, 1902**
Carved and painted redwood,
39 x 242.5 cm
*Musée d'Orsay, Paris*

**446 • The House of Pleasure: Be in
Love and You Will Be Happy, 1902**
Carved and painted redwood,
40 x 205 cm
*Musée d'Orsay, Paris*

**447 • The House of Pleasure
(left lintel), 1902**
Carved and painted redwood,
200 x 39.5 cm
*Musée d'Orsay, Paris*

**448 • The House of Pleasure
(right lintel), 1902**
Carved and painted redwood,
159 x 40 cm
*Musée d'Orsay, Paris*

**449 • Women and White Horses, 1903**
Oil on canvas, 72 x 91.5 cm
*Museum of Fine Arts, Boston*

**450 • The Invocation, 1903**
Oil on canvas, 65 x 76 cm
*National Gallery of Art, Washington*

**451 • Landscape with Dog 1903**
Oil on canvas, 72 x 91 cm

**452 • Landscape with Pig
and Horse, 1903**
Oil on canvas, 75 x 65 cm
*Ateneumin Taidemuseo, Helsinki*

**453 • Self-Portrait, 1903**
Oil on canvas mounted on wood,
42 x 25 cm
*Kunstmuseum, Basel*

# Bibliography

PAUL GAUGUIN:

*Ancien Culte mahorie,* Paris, 1951, 1967

*Avant et Après,* Paris, 1923

*Cahier pour Aline,* facsimile, Paris, 1963

*Carnet de croquis,* Paris, 1963

*Correspondance de Paul Gauguin 1873-1888,* Paris, 1984.

*Noa Noa, Voyage de Tahiti,* facsimile, Berlin, 1926 ; Paris, 1947

*Noa Noa,* facsimile, Paris, 1954 ; Paris 1966, 1988; London, 1985

*Oviri, écrits d' un sauvage, anthologie,* Paris, 1974

*Racontars de rapin,* Paris, 1951


W. ANDERSEN, *Gauguin's Paradise Lost,* New York, 1971

F. CACHIN, *Gauguin,* Paris, 1990 (French edition, 1988)

F. CACHIN, *Gauguin, "Ce malgré moi de sauvage",* Découvertes Gallimard, Paris, 1989

*Gauguin,* catalogue of the Exhibition, National Gallery of Art, Washington; The Art Institute, Chicago; Galeries nationales du Grand Palais, Paris, 1988-1989

C. GRAY, *Sculptures and Ceramics of Paul Gauguin,* Baltimore, 1963

M. HOOG, *Gauguin,* London, 1987

M. HOWARD, *Gauguin,* Gauguin Museum, Tahiti, 1993

E. KORNFELD, *Catalogue raisonné of his Prints,* Zurich, 1988

M. ROSKILL, *Van Gogh, Gauguin, and the Impressionist Circle,* Greenwich, 1970

J. DE ROTONCHAMP, *Paul Gauguin,* Paris, 1925

*Sculpture and Ceramics of Paul Gauguin,* Baltimore, 1963

G.-M. SUGANA, *Tout l'œuvre peint de Gauguin,* Paris, 1981

G. WILDENSTEIN, *Paul Gauguin,* I, Catalogue, Paris, 1964

# Picture Credits

**Agence photographique de la Réunion des Musées Nationaux, RMN**, Paris
64, 65

**AISA, Archivo Iconográfico, S.A.**, Barcelona
11, 14, 15, 20, 22, 24, 25, 26, 27, 28, 29, 30, 31, 32, 33, 34, 35, 36, 37, 38, 39, 40, 41, 42, 43, 44, 45, 46, 47, 48, 49, 50, 51, 54, 55, 56, 57, 58, 59, 60, 61, 62, 63, 70, 71, 72, 73, 74, 75, 76, 77, 78, 79, 80, 81

**Artothek**, Peissenberg
66, 67

**Giraudon**, Paris
8, 17, 18, 19, 23

**Le Musée Départemental du Prieuré**, Saint-Germain-en-Laye
7

**Museum of Fine Arts**, Boston
68, 69

**Roger-Viollet**, Paris
4, 5, 6, 9, 10

**Stadt Essen, Zentrale Museumsverwaltung**, Essen
82, 83

**The Metropolitan Museum of Art**, New York
52

**Van Gogh Museum, Vincent Van Gogh Foundation**, Amsterdam
12

The publisher wishes to express gratitude to the photographer, Alfredo Dagli Orti, for his valuable collaboration.